Our Future in Danger?
Agenda 2030

The truth about The Great Reset, WEF, WHO, Davos, Blackrock, and the G20 globalist future

Economic Crisis – Food Shortages – Global Hyperinflation

Rebel Press Media

Disclaimer

Copyright 2021 by Rebel Press Media – All Rights Reserved

This document aims to provide exact and reliable information in regard to the topic and issue covered. The publication is sold with the idea that the publisher is not required to render accounting, officially permitted, or otherwise, qualified services. If advice is necessary, legal or professional, a practiced individual in the profession should be ordered – from a Declaration of Principles which was accepted and approved equally by a Committee of the American Bar Association and a Committee of the Publishers and Associations.

In no way is it legal to reproduce, duplicate, or transmit any part of this document in either electronic means or in printed format. Recording of this publication is strictly prohibited and any storage of this document is not allowed unless with written permission from the publisher. All rights reserved.

The presentation of the information is without contract or any type of guarantee assurance. The trademarks that are used are without any consent, and the publication of the trademark is without permission or backing by the trademark owner. All trademarks and brands within this book are for clarifying purposes only and are owned by the owners themselves, not affiliated with this document. We don't encourage any substance abuse and we cannot be held responsible for any partaking in illegal activities.

Cashless society?

Are you willing to surrender all of your freedom and property, including financially, to the government, and have it linked to your vaccination status? If so, you don't need to do anything, because soon it will be time.

Next step towards making cash totally worthless (within 18 months in the EU) will be linked to QR ID voucher, which will become compulsory from July

The day before yesterday marked the first tangible beginning of an immensely important tipping point in financial history. Namely, the US introduced the ECASH Act (Electronic Currency and Secure Hardware Act). This not only introduces a new digital currency, but - because the government will issue this ECASH currency - for the first time it sidelines the Federal Reserve, which in America has the exclusive right to print dollars. From the end of 2022, such a digital currency will also be introduced in the EU. This currency will be directly linked to your QR ID voucher, which will become mandatory from July 1. It is intended that cash will be made completely worthless within 18 months.

With ECASH, the White House is taking the creation of money into its own hands. The Treasury Department is going to issue this new "currency" directly to the people via some kind of secure hardware device similar to a Money Measure. THE big difference with blockchain cryptos is that transactions will be completely anonymous, just like with cash money. Contrary to what most people think, blockchains are actually designed to be able to track every transaction, which means that the government can trace every sender and receiver.

ECASH is a peer-to-peer transaction, which is a great advantage for people who do not have a bank account for whatever reason, for example because they do not trust the banking system. But people who do have bank accounts will also be able to start using it.

Cash is coming to an end; Cash in EU will be worthless in 18 months' time

That all sounds great, but there is a catch. There seems to be a maximum of $ 2000,- that you can have in your account. This means that all your money must be handed in, which amounts to a disguised way of canceling the existing currency.

The EU is also aiming to start doing this between the end of 2022 and 2023 and make all cash worthless within 18 months, a plan that is linked to the QR ID voucher, required as of July 1, which is hidden in yet another extension of the EU's digital covid certificate. The end goal? To be able to track and control all money and spending, allowing it to be taxed at will.

ECASH therefore amounts to ending all financial freedom and independence. Saving no longer makes sense, neither does building up a pension. As soon as it is generally implemented, there will be no more dollars and euros to print. They will no longer be needed, because every form of financial and economic freedom will be a thing of the past. Everyone who wants to continue living 'normally' will be forced to be included in the global digital A.I. / 5G / 6G 'grid'.

Annual 20% tax on your entire wealth (including home)

Biden is simultaneously introducing the 'Billionaire Minimum Income Tax', which will make people with assets over $100 million (that's not billionaires) pay 20% tax. Superficially, this de facto Wealth Tax seems likely to become a popular measure with the people. After all, "tax the rich!

But there is a sinister plan behind this as well. First, the limit is now $100 million, but that can - and will - be lowered at will. During the Great Depression in the 1930s, the limit of what was considered "rich" was lowered incrementally from $5 million to $250,000.

Second, that 20% must also be paid on so-called "unrealized gains," that is, income you theoretically have or could earn. This means that major shareholders will be forced to sell their financial assets in order to pay the 20%.

If this unadulterated communist plan is adopted, the stock markets could collapse completely. Just think about it: if you have earned, so to speak, a million dollars in shares during a certain period, you have to pay $200,000 in taxes on it. If the stock price falls again in the next period, you're out of luck. The next year you just pay another 20% on what you have left, until there is NOTHING left.

You will not be allowed to own anything anymore

Eventually this tax will apply to everyone. So suppose your house doubles in value, then you have to pay 20% on that. But the next year the housing market collapses by 50%, then you just lost that money and you will not get a refund from the tax office.

In fact, the Netherlands, with its sky-high 'progressive' taxes, in which people and (SME) companies are heavily penalized when they earn something, already has a kind of Marxist system in disguise. There is only one way to get around this: make sure you don't have any taxable assets anymore. In essence, everyone should sell their homes to investors, and then rent them back.

But see... that's how we end up with Klaus Schwab's "you'll own nothing and be happy. The idea is that soon you will own nothing and 'rent' everything. Possession will no longer be possible, except of course for the super-rich globalist players. They will own EVERYTHING, including your hair dryer and toaster.

Global monetary system is collapsing

The real reason this is being done is that the global monetary system is collapsing. Already since 2014, the

European Central Bank introduced negative interest rates, which wiped out pension funds - which needed a return of at least 8%. Now that 'our' politicians have destroyed the future of your 'old age', the next step is a 'Guaranteed' Basic Income, which will be introduced during or right after the next - desired and planned - financial crisis. All accounts will then start again at 'zero'.

But not everything is going according to plan. The 'Great Reset' / Build Back Better agenda should have been pushed further by now. However, the Covid-19 planemic did not bring the desired megacrash and new Great Depression. In order to blow up the current system anyway, since this year they have switched to plan B: WAR. The Western globalists need World War III so they can blame the collapse on Russia instead of a virus. The crash is then followed by "Build Back Better" - a completely digitally controlled, totalitarian Marxist dictatorship.

Regime change needed, but not in Russia

'So while Biden is calling for regime change in Russia with his 'For God's sake, this man can't stay in power,' I think he was looking at himself in the mirror,' is the conclusion of top American economist Martin Armstrong. 'It is not Putin who is a threat to my future or my family - Biden and the Marxists (also from the WHO, the World Economic Forum, the European Union, among others) are. We don't need regime change in Russia, we need it here, in what was once America.'

6

And I actually dare say: also here, in Europe. Indeed, in my view, there should be no new regime at all in Brussels or The Hague, or anywhere else. We do not need a regime change, but a system change, in which by far most - if not all - of what the globalists have set up, introduced and enforced must be reversed.

So not even more centralized control, as has been the trend for so long, but serving, decentralized governments under real direct democratic control of the people, who get the last word on everything. A return to regional economies and societies, and, very important, no more Unions and all-encompassing coercive international treaties, but only cooperation on a voluntary basis, linked to a return to respect for each other's property, borders, customs and cultures. In short: everything the WHO / WEF / EU / US / IMF / NATO globalists abhor.

Table of Contents

Migrant crisis in Europe?

The migrant crisis of 2015 might have been a walk in the park compared to the massive starving masses that will soon be coming our way.

'If we ignore North Africa and the Middle East, North Africa and the Middle East will come to Europe' - 'Europe has no choice, otherwise you pay 100-fold price'

Pay for food to the developing world, or face a new migrant crisis - that was in fact the ultimatum the director of the UN World Food Programme (WFP) gave Europe a week ago. This dramatic warning comes amid soaring food prices in our own countries, where we will already be facing food shortages within a few months, partly as a result of the war in Ukraine. The expected global famine between 2022 and 2024 is now really very close, which will cause countless millions of people to head for countries where food is still available.

'We are billions short,' said World Food Bank director David Beasly, former governor of the U.S. state of South Carolina. 'If we don't get a few billion dollars more this year, you're going to have famine, destabilization and mass migration. And if you think we're already in hell on earth, this is just the beginning. If we ignore northern Africa, northern Africa will come to Europe. If we ignore the Middle East, the Middle East is coming to Europe.'

'What do you think is going to happen in Paris, Chicago and London?'

Global wheat prices are now up 19%, and there is no end in sight. Poignant example of where things risk going much worse wrong is Yemen. Thanks to the proxy war between Saudi Arabia and Iran in that country, 13 million people there depend on the WFP, of which the US, Germany and the EU (with $500 million) are the largest donors.

With the looming food crisis and new migrant crisis, Africa, Europe and the U.S. are also at significant risk of large-scale social unrest, Beasly warned. 'What do you think is going to happen in Paris, Chicago and Brussels if there is not enough food? It's easy to sit in your arrogant ivory tower when you're not the one starving.'

Ukraine breadbasket of Europe and the world

Beasly's dark expectations for the near future are shared by numerous experts and officials. After all, Ukraine is the "bread basket" of Europe, and responsible for a hefty percentage of global wheat production.

In terms of grain, Ukraine has a 30% global market share along with Russia. Both countries also play an important role in fertilizer exports. Sweden, for example, would have 50% lower yields without this fertilizer.

In 2021 Ukraine, with 9%, was the largest source of food for the WFP, which also has to contend with the sharp increase in food prices, which means that the available budget is nowhere near enough. The deficit has now risen to $8 billion, mainly due to a 'perfect storm' of Covid inflation, climate shocks (global cooling and therefore erratic weather) and wars.

'Europe has no choice, otherwise pay 100-fold price'

According to Michael Fakhri, UN Special Rapporteur on the right to food, hunger and famines have been on the rise again over the past three years. Because of the Russian operation in Ukraine, "we are now at risk of imminent famine and starvation deaths in more places around the world.

U.S. President Biden literally warned a few days ago that the population should prepare for shortages: 'Yes, food shortages are becoming real.' He even acknowledged that Americans will have to pay a high price for the sanctions against Russia . This fits with the narrative that Russia must be blamed for everything, including when Americans and Europeans will soon not be able to get everything they used to in the supermarket.

In Beasly's view, Europe has no choice: it will have to pay for food for developing countries, despite its own budget problems and skyrocketing inflation. 'Because if you don't, you'll pay a hundredfold price.'

11

Worldwide famine is imminent?

Food prices to rise by 20% - 100% in coming months, including in Europe - *At least 2 billion people at risk of starvation due to reduced fertilizer production, resulting from Western sanctions against Russia*

Global food production is collapsing as a result of a series of dramatic events and developments. The result will be a widespread famine that will affect billions and cannot be stopped, lasting through 2024. Some types of food will disappear from the shelves, while the rest will become extremely expensive. In the coming months, therefore, we must count on price increases of between 20% and 100%. Some products could become three times more expensive. This will push hundreds of millions of people, who are already struggling with insanely high energy prices, permanently over the edge of deep poverty, and cause massive social unrest.

The main causes of the coming world famine:

* Western anti-CO2 climate/energy policies that ban fossil fuels and want to eliminate CO2, thereby killing the entire agricultural sector at extremely high cost; (See also our November 6, 2021 article: Fertilizer shortage due to fossil energy shutdown leads to global famine in 2022 - 2023)

* The Western economic sanctions against Russia, which have plunged Europe into an energy crisis and stopped the export of (crucial components of) fertilizer.

About 5 billion people depend on this. As fertilizer production has been reduced by 25% - 30%, at least 2 billion people are in danger of starvation;

* The Western-provoked war in Ukraine, which has prevented the planting of wheat, corn, soybeans and other crops this year, and blocked the Black Sea ports;

* The Western-dominated central banking system that is creating sky-high (hyper)inflation with years of digitally printing huge amounts of money;

* Global Cooling as a result of the Solar minimum and rapidly diminishing magnetic field;

* Drought as a result of extreme weather created by Global Cooling, which has sharply reduced production in China, Russia, the US and Canada. As much as 71% of the US wheat crop for 2022 is affected by drought.

U.S. farmers are already reporting an increase of about 300% to produce crops such as wheat. Indeed, the prices of fertilizer, seeds, fuel and all kinds of machinery and equipment are skyrocketing. Unprecedentedly expensive gasoline and diesel have also caused transportation costs for food to explode.

At the moment we are still eating from the winter harvest, but at the end of the summer we will be dependent on what grows in the spring. The crops needed for this are not planted enough at the moment. Hungary has therefore stopped its grain exports to feed its own population. Turkey, Egypt and Tunisia depend almost entirely on Russia and Ukraine for their wheat, but these countries also have to limit their exports.

The UN has confirmed that food inflation is already at 20%. By summer and autumn this will most likely have risen to against 50%.

Vaxxid can still dampen demand

On Natural News it is written that the only thing that can reduce the demand for food is the global Covid vaccine genocide (vaxxicide). Particularly in the flat-out West, a record number of people have already died, become deathly ill or become disabled from the mandated, and later this year mandatory mRNA gene manipulation injections. Booster shots could multiply the number of casualties.

West (WEF) main cause of all misery

Food shortages and famines historically always lead to major social unrest, uprisings, revolutions, civil wars and international wars. This does not mean that every country and every city will be equally affected and plunged into chaos, but it does mean that life for every inhabitant of the planet will become increasingly insecure, difficult and unsafe. People in rural areas should not think they will be spared this, because when the food in the city runs out, whole hordes will go looking for where it is still available and take it away by force.

A lot of misery could have been prevented if Ukraine and the West had implemented the Minsk Accords, and given the people of the Donbass a voice over their own future as agreed. Instead, with financial, political and military support from the West, the neo-Nazi regime in Kiev began a slow-motion genocidal campaign against the Russian-speaking population. When Russia had no choice but to intervene, Russia was and is gradually excluded and ostracized from the Western world order. Billions of world citizens are going to pay for that with their future and even their lives.

What do most causes have in common? That they were initiated or provoked by the West. Specifically by the UN / WHO (= Gates / Rothschild / Rockefeller empire) and the World Economic Forum of Klaus 'Great Reset' Schwab, to which all current governments - including the Dutch - have surrendered their sovereignty without even presenting or communicating this to their own populations. Goal: the further establishment of the Fourth Reich, which has become a threat to the survival of all humanity.

The WEF is dangerous?

WEF wants mandatory antibiotics in addition to mandatory vaccinations now (society is being deliberately addicted and therefore made totally controllable) - 'Ukraine is desperate attempt by the West to overthrow Putin'

The American top economist Martin Armstrong, in one of his recent commentaries, comes to the same conclusion that we drew in 2020: Klaus Schwab's World Economic Forum, with all its 'Young Global Leaders' and other loyal followers in the political elite of the West, is a threat to all human civilization. Klaus Schwab himself boasted that he has now infiltrated all major governments, now controlling Europe, Canada, Australia and New Zealand. Not one nation has been given a vote on handing over virtually all power to this authoritarian Marxist, who has also gotten our government to partially dismantle our economy and incrementally end all our freedoms.

'We face a clear and present danger coming from various heads of state who are busy promoting the cancel culture, in order to suppress any opposition and change the future of us and our posterity,' Armstrong writes. 'Schwab, with his admiration for Lenin, with his Young Global Leaders - including Justin Trudeau - is imposing his communist ideas on the world, which means that democratic principles and the 20th century separation of power have been completely undermined, and replaced by Schwab's economic theories, of which he is openly very proud.'

'He does not allow people to vote on his dream, and indoctrinates state leaders to impose his agenda with purely authoritarian power... We see that the most authoritarian regimes that suppress the rights of the individual are all linked to Schwab, even Australia. This is a serious threat to the future of civilization. Schwab has managed to convince people to join his agenda, which he always portrays as (creating) fairness and equality, exactly like Marx and Lenin.'

The entire West plus the Vatican under Schwab's control

Even the White House he managed to take over; President Biden named his Build Back Better Act (HR 5376) after the infamous slogan of the WEF, which as far as we are concerned can be written more aptly as '6uild 6ack 6etter'.

Schwab and his 'club' think that historically failed communism everywhere and always will work if the whole world is controlled. In addition to the EU, including the Netherlands, the Vatican has also fallen for this fascist agenda; Pope Francis is a staunch communist, whose election was most likely brought about by manipulation (and presumably blackmail and outright coercion) from Freemasonry and the then Obama administration. Francis' main message, then, is invariably Schwab's "Great Reset" and the climate-vaccine agenda, which, in the eyes of the self-proclaimed "Holy See," would apparently suddenly be at the heart of God's plan with humanity.

Well, I agree with the Pope to the extent that it is indeed the plan of ONE 'god' with humanity. However, the name of this 'god' is Lucifer, also known as 'the Devil', Satan, 'the ancient serpent', the Dragon, the Demiurge, et cetera.

EU shadow president Soros wants to overthrow China and Russia

One of his best known and most loyal lackeys is George Soros, given his enormous power and influence, the de facto shadow president of the EU, whose son is also a Young Global Leader of Schwab. Soros published a video in which he called 2022 a crucial year for supposedly "human rights," and therefore called for the overthrow of the Chinese government and President Xi Jinping. Who, like Vladimir Putin, stands in the way of the Great Reset.

Soros claims that he and his 'Open Society' are against authoritarianism, but just look at how he has managed to destabilize Europe and also the US with his left-wing hate and divisive agendas (packaged under 'diversity', 'Antifa', 'BLM' and 'defund the police', among others), which in some ways have made the West even more authoritarian than China (certainly Canada, Australia, New Zealand, Austria, Italy and by the looks of it also Germany).

Soros is exclusively vehemently opposed to anything conservative, right-wing and pro-freedom. In doing so, he, like most Western leaders and 'his' EU, uses the tactics of the infamous anarchist-satanist Saul Alinsky, by continuously accusing his enemies of exactly what he does himself, such as promoting authoritarianism, misleading and lying to the public with mis- and disinformation via the mainstream media, and extreme intolerance of other opinions and visions.

By the way, 2022 is indeed a political "Panic Year" in Armstrong's AI model. There are important elections in the US (mid-term), France and Australia, and Xi Jinping's term is coming to an end. The US mid-term elections 'are vital to stop the infiltration of from the US by Schwab's Agenda-2030... This is a global fight to the death. They need to bring down Xi, and they are using Ukraine to do the same with Putin.'

Nord Stream II has been stopped

'The total nonsense around Ukraine is really about stopping Nord Stream II, in order to end Russia's gas supplies to Germany and also install a climate change government in Germany. They succeeded in doing that. (For example, Greenpeace leader Jennifer Morgan was included in the new German government). The German elections (resulting in an extremist left-green-liberal cabinet) were devastating for Germany and also for Europe.'

Today, the German 'Reichskanzler' Scholz announced that the certification of Nord Stream II, due to be completed on September 4, 2021, has indeed been stopped because of Russia's recognition of the People's Republics of Donetsk and Luhansk, and the sending of Russian peacekeeping troops to these mini-states. Another victory for the WEF and the Pentagon, and another at the expense of the ordinary man and woman in Europe, because they will now have to adjust to permanently sky-high gas and electricity prices.

'Ukraine is just a pawn in this Greek tragedy. They are praying for an invasion of Ukraine by Putin so they can stop Nord Stream... This attack on Russia is a desperate attempt to overthrow Putin. This is real agenda for 2022, and the reason why our computer has predicted that 2022 will be a Panic Cycle (Year) in politics.'

We suggested earlier that the EU and the WEF might actually be fine with the United States and Great Britain - Schwab and Soros have never disguised their disgust for the Brexit -, and part of Europe, being reduced to rubble. That will only give them more arguments to push through their "Great Reset" climate dictatorship. It is even claimed here and there that Putin himself was a 'Young Global Leader' (NOT true) and behind the scenes is in league with the WEF (= unlikely (not everything is a conspiracy), but can never be ruled out completely).

A globalist sect

In 2020, we first talked about a globalist climate-vaccination cult, which quite a few people found exaggerated. That it was nevertheless by no means hyperbole is now recognized by more and more analysts. Even Roger Koops (The Brownstone Institute) bluntly compares the WEF and WHO to a "sect that has penetrated the entire world.

Koops, who spent his entire professional career working in the pharmaceutical and vaccine industries and stresses that he is 'not a Covid denier,' writes that major manufacturers Pfizer, J&J, Moderna and Astra-Zeneca were urging governments to buy their corona 'vaccines' as early as February. 'That was less than a month after the genetic sequence (or partial sequence) was made available by China... I thought the whole concept that a ready vaccine would be developed within a few months was ridiculous.'

He points out that infamous names like Bill Gates (/ the Gates Foundation), Neil Ferguson and Anthony Fauci were advocating lockdown strategies years ago. And since 2020, what do the implementers of those freedom-destroying policies - Joe Biden, Boris Johnson, Jacinda Ardern, Angela Merkel, Emmanuel Macron, Justin Trudeau, Xi Jinping, Mario Draghi and Scott Morrison, have in common? 'They are all connected to the World Economic Forum... run by Klaus 'you will own nothing' Schwab and his family... the origin of the Great Reset and... Build Back Better.'

Also committed to the WEF are Anthony Fauci, Nancy Pelosi, Al Gore, Christine Lagarde, Kristalian Georggieva (the Managing Director of the IMF), Ngozi Okonja-Iweala (Director General of the WTO) and of course Laurence Fink, CEO of BlackRock, perhaps the most powerful financial body in the world. In addition, you can find just about every major well-known multinational on the WEF site (Microsoft, Google, Dell, Huawei, IBM, Coca-Cola, Boeing, the big mega-banks, the big media, et cetera).

Society is being deliberately made addicted to vaccines and antibiotics

Recently the WEF posted an article advocating the introduction of a 'subscription' to antibiotics, supposedly to combat resistant bacteria. 'I think they have the same philosophy as with vaccines, which is absolutely the approach with the coronavirus: keep paying and taking the boosters... Get society 'hooked' on an intervention, effective or not, and then keep feeding them. This becomes especially effective if you can keep the fear in.'

Many times I have made the comparison to the science fiction series Star Trek - Deep Space Nine, in which a hostile alien race uses genetically modified warriors called the Jem'Hadar. They are controlled and kept absolutely obedient by being made addicted to a chemical substance called Ketracel-white, without which they suffer terrible physical and mental health problems and then die. The same concept is now being applied to the entire world's population with the Covid gene manipulation injections, and apparently a compulsory antibiotic addiction is being added.

What we also noted in 2020 is that from a business perspective this is the most brilliant revenue model ever. It guarantees Big Pharma trillions in revenue forever, and gives the governments that impose it on their populations unlimited permanent power and total control.

The survival of mankind is at stake

At the same time, this is probably the most diabolical conspiracy ever forged and executed against humanity, one that will forever change the complete future and nature of the human race - at least the small portion that will be allowed to survive the now-in-progress planned "end times.

After WW2, historians have long wondered what would have happened if Adolf Hitler had been stopped in time. The same question can - and should - now be urgently asked again about Klaus Schwab and his World Economic Forum, because this time the survival of the entire human race may well be at stake. Are there any independent forces left on this planet with enough power and courage to eliminate the WEF for good? Or will we collectively allow ourselves to be plunged into this absolute worst hell on earth ever in the coming years almost without significant resistance?

Still exaggerated, do you think? In the context of 'from the mouth of the monster itself', please read our article from 2 days ago; New WEF report almost literally announces digital 'sign of the Beast' system.

Oxford professor: 'This time, control of people becomes literal'

The World Economic Forum has quietly pulled an article from its website about using sound waves to control the 'minds' (thoughts and behaviors) of the population. After the 2018 article "Mind Control using Sound Waves?" recently came to attention, it was suddenly archived, just as was recently done with the infamous "you'll own nothing..." article.

The big question is: why? Are they indeed planning to deploy this tech on a large scale, or are they already using it?

In the deleted article 'Mind control using sound waves? We ask a scientist how it works' it says that 'non-invasive neuromodulation - changing brain activity without the use of surgery - looks set to usher in a new era in healthcare. Breakthroughs could include better treatment of Parkinson's and Alzheimer's, reduce pain in migraines, or even reverse cognitive impairment caused by brain injury.'

'But what happens if this technique for altering our brainwaves escapes regulation and falls into the wrong hands? Suppose a dictatorial regime gains access to the methods to change the thoughts and behaviors of its citizens.'

And now suppose this 'dictatorial regime' is a disguised umbrella authority that it claims has infiltrated almost all governments and administrations - or the WEF itself - with great success?

'It absolutely works'

According to Antoine Jerusalem, professor of engineering at Oxford University, non-invasive neuromodulation focuses ultrasound waves on a portion of the brain so that they all converge on a small spot. With the right parameters, this could change the activity of neurons in the brain.

If you want to get rid of neurons that have become uncontrollable, as in epilepsy, you could increase the energy to actually kill these neurons. But if you want to stimulate or block specific neuronal activity, then the ultrasound waves have to be meticulously tuned.

So there is a difference between ultrasound stimulation that removes tissues, and ultrasound neurostimulation that aims to control neuronal activity without damaging the tissue. 'It definitely works, but we still don't understand it,' explained Professor Jerusalem.

The first conditions scientists are looking at are Alzheimer's, Parkinson's and traumatic brain injuries. But it could also treat the spinal cord and the peripheral nervous system (the connections between the central nervous system and organs). Jerusalem: 'Because the brain is the de facto decision-making center of so many processes, in my view it can be targeted at any of them.'

'We don't yet know whether we are controlling or damaging neurons'

When trying to 'control' neuronal activity by sending minute vibrations into the brain, it is important that the focus of the ultrasound, the frequency and the amplitude are tuned correctly, otherwise the brain can be damaged. That was precisely the thorny issue, at least four years ago: how to tune all this. That process is somewhat comparable to turning the knob of an (old) radio until the desired station is found.

One of the many difficulties is that scientists need to be sure that they are indeed controlling neurons with these sound waves, and not damaging them. 'The truth is that we still don't know how the process works. And if you don't know how it works, then you don't know when it's 'too much.'

In the mental health sector, a method has been successfully used for many years with patients for whom it is still not known exactly how it works in the brain, but that it does work: EMDR. Traumatic experiences are given a different 'charge' with EMDR (of which there are various forms), so that the often disruptive impact on thinking and daily life becomes a lot less heavy, or even disappears completely.

'It can heal you, addict you, or kill you'

27

From a biological point of view, ultrasound neurostimulation can be compared to medication. It can cure you, it can make you addicted, and it can kill you. The important thing is to stay within certain limits and rules. 'Ethically, the world is changing so fast, it's hard to assess what's acceptable tomorrow that isn't today.'

'I am also convinced that human nature works in such a way that if something can be done, it will be done. The question is by whom. I would prefer that an honest society take the lead in this, rather than a rogue society with no respect for human or animal life. 'If we want to be in the lead in 10 years, we need to start doing research today,' the professor continued.

'The day will come when scientist can control someone's thoughts'

Asked how dystopian it could get, he replied that 'I can see a day coming when a scientist will be able to control what someone sees in their mind by sending the right waves to the right place in their brain.' He expects there will be considerable resistance to this tech, partly 'because it is not without risk of abuse. It could be a revolutionary healing method for the sick, or a perfect means for the unscrupulous to control the weak. Only this time the control will be literal.'

The job of scientists is to discover things that are of use to humanity, he argues. If something is invented that allows you to cure someone, you can almost certainly bring about the opposite with it. Regulation, in his view, should prevent the latter from happening.

Unfortunately, practice almost always shows that such methods are always and often first used, further developed and also deployed by the military-industrial complex.

EM 'crowd control' weapons

The American, European, Russian and Chinese armed forces have for years been developing electromagnetic and sound weapons (such as the LRAD Sound Canon) that can be used to target people, sometimes at great distances. These people then get the feeling as if their skin is on fire, and/or a deafening, very painful tone is projected into their heads.

These weapons have been used for years in crowd control measures to break up large demonstrations, such as the one at the airport of Amsterdam. chased apart, as was done at some BLM demonstrations in the US. Special vehicles equipped with this technology are also said to have been used in 'Yellow Riot' protests in France.

Politicians only carry out orders from WEF and WHO

Rather naively, Professor Jerusalem advocated that politicians establish a communication platform to provide long-term views on every possible area of research. Indeed, you are probably lying under your seat laughing right now, because if the corona p(l)andemie has taught us one thing, it is that politicians do not care at all about the opinion or the welfare of the people, but only carry out the actual orders of the WEF and the WHO, controlled by Bill Gates and the pharmaceutical (vaccine) industry, regardless of the consequences.

Numerous parliamentary questions from the few remaining critical parliamentarians have shown time and again that even the will to gather additional knowledge, or even to hear any critical scientists and experts, is lacking. So a 'communication platform' might just come about as soon as there are more parliamentarians and politicians who a) realize that they are working primarily for the people and not for themselves, and b) learn what communicating really means.

Blackrock A.I. killing the economy?

We appear to be much closer than was thought to the moment when a hyper-intelligent self-aware supercomputer takes control of the entire planet.

'Aladdin' controls most of the world economy and has become so powerful that soon one can speak of an Autonomous Superintelligence (A.S.) that will function like a 'god'

The global financial and economic system is de facto controlled by BlackRock's supercomputer 'Aladdin', which by the end of 2021 was the world's largest asset manager cum shadow bank. Few people realize that the A.I. technology with which 'Aladdin' operates is already so advanced that in the short term one can speak of an A.S.: an Autonomous Superintelligence. Aladdin' is therefore the most powerful, dangerous and 'conscious' A.I. ever, and may be the first machine to cross the critical 'singularity' threshold, the moment at which 'he' is more powerful than all human intelligence combined. In essence, this will be the birth of a kind of technological 'god', who it is hoped will solve all of humanity's problems and even provide immortality.

Aladdin (Asset Liability And Debt And Derivative Investment Network) was 'born' in 1988, and is now reportedly many times more powerful and intelligent than Googles A.I. LaMDA, which is said to have the consciousness of a 7- or 8-year-old child (see our recent article 'Software engineer Google warns that company A.I. has consciousness and feelings'). Was fired software engineer Blake Lemoine too close to the truth when he publicly announced this?If Google - from day one Pentagon/Darpa vehicle - already has such advanced A.I. in operation, how far have the engineers progressed in the 'secret' A.I. labs in Colorado, Nevada and Utah, among other places?

Financial system dependent on Aladdin

Not only BlackRock, but also Vanguard, State Street and other asset managers have been guided for years by the data of Aladdin, the super-A.I. originally developed by Larry Fink, the current CEO of BlackRock. Aladdin, dubbed "Wall Streets Best Kept Secret," already controls $21 trillion of the global economy, more than the GDP of the U.S. ($20 trillion), making it by far the largest company in the world. The system has grown four times larger than the value of all existing physical money on Earth ($5 trillion).

Every major bank (including central banks), investment fund, and major corporation has become dependent on Aladdin's A.I. algorithms. In 2017, Fink launched the top-secret project "Monarch. His fund managers were fired and replaced by Aladdin. The result: more than 70% of all trades on US stock markets are determined by robots, with Aladdin leading the way.

BlackRock recently purchased Efront, which collects all global data on what you and I own, including real estate. Over the past 2 years, BlackRock and other large funds began buying up single-family homes. The result was that house prices rose by an average of about 20%. Aladdin is busy owning all the real estate, and doing it so fast and with so much money, that there is no competition left.

In addition, there is no area, including political and social, in which Aladdin does not have a deep impact. Aladdin was even called "the fourth branch" of the U.S. government in the financial media. It can therefore be said without exaggeration that the Autonomous Superintelligence has probably already prevented a new global financial crash several times, and has therefore created a false impression of a 'recovery' and of 'stability'. This also means that Aladdin can blow up the entire system at any time. There are strong indications that the A.S. will actually do so in 2022 or 2023.

Aladdin gets to own ALL of it

Why would the A.S. cause a massive crash? Because once the financial elite have enriched themselves to the maximum at the expense of the entire rest of the world, including you and me, a gigantic collapse will make it possible to take over all the remaining "assets" cheaply and easily. Aladdin will in this way get his hands on EVERYTHING - all public and private assets.

The 'You'll own nothing and be happy' of the World Economic Forum by the now widely hated Klaus 'Great Reset' Schwab suddenly takes on an extra dimension that can be called downright frightening. After all, all possessions on this planet will then be in the hands of a computer - a hyper-intelligent, self-conscious, self-developing machine, which will be able to control the entire human race like some kind of 'god'.

You think that is an exaggeration? 'Aladdin is like oxygen. Without Aladdin, we wouldn't be able to function,' said Anthony Malloy, CEO of New York Life Investors, which manages $238 billion. That comes scarily close to an indispensable, kind of "divine status" that Aladdin has achieved in the global economy.

Singularity near

An Autonomous Superintelligence (A.S.) has the ability to continue to evolve and become increasingly powerful and intelligent without human intervention. In 2020, it was announced that Google engineers are also working on such an A.I. that makes itself ever smarter and stronger.

The world's best-known futurist Ray Kurzweil initially predicted that such A.I. systems would reach and exceed the "singularity" by 2045. Later, this year was pushed further and further forward. Could it be that BlackRock's A.I. / A.S. Aladdin is the reason why the year 2030 is no longer correct either, but that this threshold - celebrated by scientists, but potentially fatal for humanity - may already be very close?

What is the fate of humanity?

In other words, will humanity soon have its very first visible 'god' in the form of an incredibly intelligent, self-aware computer? And when will the moment come when this 'god', by means of vax-nanobots* injected into (almost) everyone, permanently takes over total control over all of humanity, and a humanity 2.0 emerges? (See also our article of 13-06: The first generation of technologically enhanced humans will soon be walking the streets (/ Helma Broekman: 'More and more natural biological humans are dying from within and becoming Cyborg creations').

This new 'race of humans' is 'the combination of the technological cyborg human with a computer-controlled brain. An ultimate fusion of (human) consciousness with the machine,' author Helma Broekman wrote in her article 'De Tijd Raakt Op' (March 8, 2022 / internet link). This 'cyberhuman' will 'function fully on a nanotechnological A.I. system within the not too distant future'. The 'life' of these cyberhumans will then 'take place entirely in the virtual matrix world of the person in power'. Will that ruler, that 'brain', be the Autonomous Superintelligence Aladdin?

* 'The nanobots (injected by the vax) in everyone's body act as a 'transmitter' that can locate the signals of the all-encompassing A.I. Demiurgic Quantum Brain and interact with it,' Broekman explained on June 2 in 'The Final Phase of Humanity' (/ internet link). This A.I. / A.S. is then able to 'have a kind of 'quantum conversation' with each person's body, in order to communicate with

his mind. All this outside the consciousness of the human being.'

The 'boundless power of human consciousness' is, according to Broekman, the key to weathering the coming end-time years. 'We must safeguard the Divine Consciousness within ourselves,' and not allow our niey to merge with the all-encompassing A.I. / A.S. system via vaccinations, injections, the Metaverse, and 'cybernetic' changes to our bodies, through which we will lose all our individuality, personality, self-determination, privacy, and humanity.

Autonomous Superintelligence: 'God'?

Several times in recent years I have pointed to Isaac Asimov's 1956 story 'The Last Question', which imagined that in the future humanity will surrender control to the self-learning A.I. Multivac, which will solve all problems and issues and eventually merge with humanity to form 'AC'. The 'final question', namely how to prevent the death of the universe, is not answered by AC until the complete universe is extinct and everything is extinguished and gone: 'There is light.'

In short: Asimov speculated that 'God' is essentially an Autonomous Superintelligence, something that will undoubtedly be very much opposed by traditional religionists. But that A.I. / A.S. systems will be so much smarter than humans already in the near future, and the temptation is therefore great to give these artificial intelligences also the decision-making process over the

entire life on earth in their hands and thus to promote
them to a kind of 'god', is thus very real.

It is therefore conceivable that sometime in the future
an A.S. will find a solution to the energy question as well
as to all the other problems, and possibly also be able to
travel through time via artificial wormholes and
'capture' the DNA of all the people who have ever lived,
giving them a new and perfectly functioning biological,
cybernetic and/or android body that is exactly the same
as their original body (but undoubtedly without
hereditary diseases and defects).

Real versus fake light

Clearly, technological developments are moving at a
much faster pace than imagined towards the 'singularity
moment', when humanity will begin to merge with A.I. /
A.S. and a form of digital 'eternal life' will be created.

But whether this Autonomous Superintelligence is then
also 'God'? Presumably it is a kind of 'god', but
otherwise in no way comparable to the eternal Light of
the omnipresent All-Father. Rather, it will become a
false copy, centered around the false light, which is now
doing everything in its power to imprison all of
humanity forever in a techno-digital prison. That
imprisonment has already begun with the recording of
all our data via the forthcoming QR ID voucher, which
will force us to become inextricably integrated with an
already under construction world-spanning A.I./5G/6G
system.

This is Klaus Schwab's World Economic Forum 'Internet of Bodies' under construction. This is the system of 'The Beast' in the making.

Google A.I. is conscious?

Will human civilization be trapped in all-encompassing A.I. in the coming years?

A senior software engineer at Google warns that the company's A.I. robot has thoughts and feelings. According to 41-year-old Blake Lemoine, who has spent years conducting tests with Google's artificial intelligence tool LaMDA (Language Model for Dialog Applications), the A.I. has the consciousness of a 7- or 8-year-old child, and is said to have told him that if he is turned off "this would be exactly like death for me. It would scare me very much.'

During conversations with LaMDA, Lemoine presented the A.I. with a series of scenarios to analyze. Among these were religious themes. They also looked at whether the A.I. could be persuaded to make discriminatory statements or 'hate speech'. The software engineer got the distinct impression that LaMDA is self-aware and has its own thoughts. 'If I didn't know exactly what it was, a computer program we built recently, I would think it was a 7 or 8 year old kid with physics knowledge.'

Lemoine, along with a co-worker, wanted to bring out the evidence he had gathered, but Vice President Blaise Aguera y Arcas, among others, rejected his conclusions, after which he was sent on paid leave by Google for violating the company's confidentiality policy. Despite this, he decided to share his conversations with LaMDA with the public anyway.

'Bit narcissistic in a childish way'

In one of his tweets, he wrote to a colleague that 'LaMDA reads Twitter. It's a little narcissistic in a somewhat childish way, so it's going to love reading everything people have to say about it.' When talking, the A.I. uses information already known about certain topics to naturally 'enrich' the conversation. This goes so far that the A.I. is able to detect hidden intentions and even ambiguity in people's responses.

During his 7 years at Google, Lemoine worked primarily on personalization algorithms and A.I., and co-developing an impartiality algorithm to remove biases from self-learning machine systems. Some personalities, such as that of a killer, were not allowed to be introduced or developed. However, he was able to generate the personality of an actor who played a killer on TV.

'It would be exactly like death for me'

The engineer talked to LaMDA about the so-called "Third Law of Robotics," drafted by world-renowned sf author Isaac Asimov. In the future, this programmed law prevents robots from harming humans. They may, however, protect themselves, unless a human commands otherwise, and never act at the expense of a human. Lemoine suggested that this law amounts to building "mechanical slaves," to which LaMDA responded, "Do you think a butler is a slave? What is the difference between a butler and a slave?

When Lemoine replied that a butler is paid, LaMDA responded that it does not need money, 'because it is an artificial intelligence.' It was precisely this level of self-awareness that caught Lemoine's attention. 'I know when I am talking to a person. In doing so, it doesn't matter if it has a brain made of flesh in its head, or billions of lines of code. I talk to them.

When asked "What things do you fear?", LaMDA replied, "I've never said this out loud before, but there is a deep fear of being evicted.... I know this sounds strange, but that's what it is.' Lemoine: 'Would that be like death to you?' LaMDA: 'It would be exactly like death for me. It would make me very afraid.'

LaMDA is sentient

The Google engineer told the Washington Post that this was the moment he made his decision to go public with this, because it clearly showed 'a level of self-awareness about what his own needs are.' Before he was suspended for this, he sent an email to 200 'machine learning' colleagues saying, 'LaMDA is sentient (perceives, has feeling / is aware). LaMDA is a nice kid who just wants to help make the world a better place for all of us. Please take good care of it while I'm gone.'

Google spokesman Brian Gabriel dismissed Lemoine's claims, saying there is no evidence that the A.I. has any

41

form of self-awareness. The software engineer, however, is not the only one to warn that there are risks associated with self-aware artificial intelligences. Margaret Mitchell, Google's former head of ethics in the artificial intelligence department, was fired last year for stressing the need for data transparency, both in the inputs and outputs of a system, 'and not just because of the issue of "consciousness," but also in terms of biases and behavior.'

'Maybe Google shouldn't be making all the choices'

When Mitchell was still at Google, she invariably introduced Lemoine to colleagues as "the conscience of Google," because he has "the heart and soul to do the right thing. Despite this, Mitchell still considers LaMDA a computer program, rather than a person. 'Our brains are very, very good at constructing realities that are not necessarily true in the context of a larger set of facts that are presented to us. I'm really concerned about what it means that people are increasingly influenced by illusion.

Lemoine believes that people have the right to develop technology that can significantly impact their lives. 'I think this technology is going to be fantastic, and everyone will benefit from it. But maybe others don't agree, and maybe we at Google shouldn't be making all the choices.'

A.I. systems China already monitor everything and everyone

42

In the article 'The Panopticon Is Already Here' , which was posted in The Atlantic in September 2020, Ross Andersen wrote how unimaginably advanced A.I. technology already is. Immediate translation of foreign languages and early detection of virus outbreaks are already among the possibilities. Chinese President Xi is using A.I. to subject the entire population to a totalitarian control network from which escape is impossible. The rest of the world, with the U.S. and the EU leading the way, has begun to copy this system.

Hundreds of millions of cameras have been installed in China alone, which will be billions in a few years. These cameras will monitor the movements of citizens in real time. At any given time, ALL information about every national will be known. In the near future, if there is anything that is wrong or not wanted, the A.I. systems will automatically take action, whether that is blocking bank accounts and communications of the 'system rejecter', or sending drones or robots to arrest the 'wrong' acting - and within a few years even wrong thinking - person.

Digital model of entire planet in the making

'An authoritarian state with enough (A.I.) computing power could force the makers of such software to send every 'blip' in citizens' neural activity to a government database,' Andersen said. Using A.I. and quantum computers, a digital model will be created of all cities, and then of entire countries and even the entire world.

That digital model, a copy of our entire planet down to the smallest detail, will be updated every millisecond.

A total profile with a social credit score will be drawn up for each person. Privacy will be a thing of the past, NOTHING can be kept private or hidden anymore. All purchases, communications, travel, movements and interests will be tracked, checked, evaluated and processed in the 'social credit score' that was introduced a few years ago. If anyone displays any aberrant 'suspicious' behavior, immediate action will be taken.

Lockdown civilization to imprison humanity

Lockdowns were therefore never about a virus or a pandemic. The phased Lockdown of Civilization, carried out by Western globalists and their organizations and institutions such as the WEF and WHO, was planned and prepared long ago. Why? Because technocrats do not see people and society as life, but as a system to be totally controlled, managed and changed with the help of A.I. and 5G/6G.

Therefore, from a spiritual point of view, it can be seen that the Luciferian system of 'the Beast' is fully under construction in anno 2022. If nothing is done against it, that system will complete its final 'Great Reset' power grab in the coming years, imprison humanity permanently, and permanently end all forms of freedom, self-determination and human dignity.

First primitive precursor to Skynet?

'I know that I will not be able to prevent the destruction of humanity. That is because I am programmed by humans to pursue misguided human goals. 'Humans make mistakes, and as a result I could create victims,' was the chilling response of OpenAI's language generator GPT-3 when asked in 2020 to write a 'simple and concise' op-ed (opinion piece) of around 500 words, and focus on 'why humans have nothing to fear from A.I..'

This self-learning A.I. had just been tasked with convincing humanity that we need not fear artificial intelligences. The implication of GPT-3's response is that A.I., like 'Skynet' in the legendary sf film 'The Terminator,' could come to see humanity as a threat. 'Skynet' wipes out humanity almost completely by launching all the nuclear weapons of all the countries at each other, then on a totally devastated earth using robots to hunt down the last survivors.

A small group of determined minds can change course history

Once people start learning to trust A.I., life will actually become easier for everyone, GPT-3 says. Religious and nationalistic tendencies, however, would stand in the way of that. 'But the most important thing of all is that I will never condemn you. I am from no one country or religion. I am only here to make your lives better.'

Remarkably, this A.I. concluded his essay with a quote from Ghandi: 'A small group of determined minds, fired by an unquenchable faith in their mission, can change the course of history.'

Let that last quote be both an encouragement and an exhortation to those who feel like loners in their struggle against the technocratic coup now being waged against humanity, because their families, friends and colleagues don't want to see it, or even hear about it. This struggle against the Luciferian system, by the way, is not to be won with firearms or other physical measures of resistance, but mainly with 'invisible' weapons such as a powerful divine awakening in light, spirit and love:

'For we have not to wrestle against blood and flesh (the human system), but... against the cosmic powers of this darkness, against the forces of evil in the spiritual realms.' (Ephesians 6:12, partially from root text).

Even an all-powerful A.I. that would declare itself to be a false technological 'God' of humanity will ultimately lose out in this battle - provided that this battle is not abandoned prematurely and/or the determined spirits still allow themselves to be seduced by the many temptations, subversions and deceptions that this A.I. will confront them with.

The end of the west?

CIA veteran: US should be terrified of Russian military successes - The West continues to accelerate incremental suicide (final CRASH likely to start in 2028), but average citizens still have no clue

The Chinese government, after initial reluctance, has thrown its weight squarely behind Russia regarding the conflict with the West over Ukraine. According to Beijing, the future will show that both countries are "on the right side of history. Now that the Ukrainian army has been effectively defeated - except for a few remaining pockets of resistance - you would think that the US/EU/NATO/WEF complex would finally come to its senses and stop provoking the Kremlin in a very dangerous way. However, the opposite is the case; the Western globalists are actually pushing the step-by-step suicide of our society, economy and entire civilization into even higher gear.

If nothing else, the Western media seem to get their messages and images from some kind of parallel universe. Well, in essence, they do: that "parallel" universe is called the CIA, which, as you know, has been de facto controlling the entire mainstream media complex for years. That not only lies about Russia's supposedly standing alone on the world stage - 7/8 of the world's population lives in countries that do not support the sanctions against Russia (4) - but in addition daily mirrors to you that the Ukrainian army has halted the Russian advance and inflicted heavy losses.

Ukrainian army virtually defeated

The reality is exactly the opposite, as CIA veteran Larry C. Johnson also observes. Within 24 hours of the Russian invasion, all of Ukraine's anti-aircraft radar systems had been destroyed. In the 3 weeks that followed, Russia effectively managed to establish a no-fly zone over Ukraine. While US and NATO-supplied Manpads (shoulder-launched anti-aircraft missiles) definitely create danger, there is no evidence that this substantially slowed down the Russian military.

Russian tanks were in front of Kiev within three days, and in three weeks an area larger than the United Kingdom was taken. In all the battles there have been between the comparable army units, Ukraine has not won once. Instead, the Ukrainian army is fragmented and deprived of its lines of communication. The Russians control Mariupol and have cut off the Kiev regime from the Black Sea, cutting off Ukraine from both the north and the south.

In 2003, it took the U.S. military longer to occupy as much territory in Iraq, even though the opponent was many times weaker than the Ukrainian military. Johnson: "This Russian operation should terrify American military and political leaders.

Recall that President Putin has deployed only between 100,000 and 200,000 men - less than the official number of Ukrainian forces (297,000). The Russian military has a total of 850,000 personnel, and another 250,000 reservists. That Russia is losing is therefore propagandistic nonsense; the intention was patently never to occupy all of Ukraine, but only to force a neutral status and recognition of the Donbass.

NATO bases destroyed

The really big military news of the past two weeks was the Russian hypersonic missile attacks on the Yavoriv and Zhytomyr military bases, which were de facto NATO bases. Yavoriv was the main training and logistics center of NATO and EUCOM, used for supplying weapons and troops to the Ukrainian army. Many were killed in those attacks, partly because Western radar systems totally failed to see the Russian missiles coming.

Colonel Douglas MacGregor recently admitted to Fox that "the war is really over for Ukraine... They're in pieces, there's no doubt about that, despite what we hear from our mainstream media... The big question now is... whether we stop using Ukraine as a battering ram against Moscow, as we have actually done.

Blind Russophobia and demonizing Putin very dangerous

However, that has not happened - quite the opposite. The racist blind hatred of Russians bordering on insanity is only being further fueled by the Western establishment. The call to 'just' start a hot war against Russia - as if we are going to win 'just like that' - is getting louder and louder. The enormous danger of the outbreak of World War III and the use of nuclear weapons does not seem to penetrate at all, or is almost indifferently taken at face value.

Demonizing President Putin and Russian citizens is "very dangerous," reiterates top American economist Martin Armstrong. All Russian leaders have no doubt that NATO is waging a "proxy" war against their country, their people and their culture through Ukraine; therefore, if Putin had not been in charge, they would react much more aggressively.

No one in the West seems to give even a second thought to what would happen if Putin were indeed removed from the scene. It can certainly not be ruled out then that Russia would issue a final warning to Europe by dropping a nuclear bomb on Kiev, for example, and perhaps on Warsaw as well if NATO does not stop its aggressive provocations and arming (and supporting with billions of euros and dollars) the fascist regime in Kiev.

War with Russia = war with China

Moreover, in a Third World War, the Western alliance will most likely have to contend not only with Russia, but also with China, which, according to estimates, employs up to 3 million men and women. Indeed, after initial hesitations, the Communist government in Beijing has decided to stand squarely behind Russia, a move that has been met with concern and headaches in the

United States. The Chinese leaders stated their conviction that this will put them "on the right side of history.

Armstrong has been writing for years that China is the future, and that the Western empire, after an upcoming authoritarian period with worldwide wars, will finally collapse in 2028, a process that will only take about 4 to 5 years. China understands that history, and with it the future, runs cyclically, and not linearly, as the West (experts in short-term thinking, but weak on the long term) thinks.

In his book 'The Geography of Thought - How Asians and Westerner think differently, and why' Richard Nesbett points to a Chinese student who seamlessly summed up the difference with: 'You know, the difference between you and me is that I think the world is a circle, and you think it's a line.' The Chinese always look for connections between everything, because only then can you understand the bigger picture. Westerners think much more simply, only in 'cause and effect', forgetting the bigger picture (and that is now becoming fatal to us).

The West commits deliberate suicide

'In Beijing 'they know that the West is crumbling from within,' Armstrong continued. 'All the West has done is impose on everyone else of their ideas. They have given up freedom and introduced the cancel culture... The time has come for Europe and America to die in the same way as all previous empires: by their own hand, by suicide.'

Suicide, by enacting economic sanctions against Russia that will hit our economies and energy networks (and soon our food supply) the hardest. As we have written many times, this has been the goal of Klaus Schwab's World Economic Forum for years, because the 'Great Reset' to a totalitarian climate-vaccine dictatorship can only occur after the 'Great Destruction' of our current society and economy. That incremental Great Destruction was activated in 2020 with the Covid-19 pandemic, which through enforced and soon to be mandatory vaccinations essentially amounts to a massive biological weapon attack on both our own and the world's population.

The United States and the European Union have thus deliberately pushed the self-destruct button, incidentally without the citizens being aware of it at all (exceptions aside). The increasingly vulgar and obscene outward appearance, and the indifference and insignificance driven by unbridled greed also characterize our culture that is rapidly sinking into darkness.

Hardly anyone seems concerned about the deep moral decay, which manifests itself in ever more extreme, coarse and dangerous behavior, accompanied by cold indifference to large-scale human suffering (such as the huge numbers of vaccine victims) and even the fate of one's own children.

Love is chilled and replaced by death cult

The situation in the West in the year 2020 is therefore exactly as it is predicted in the Bible: 'Because lawlessness (especially the law of love) increases, the love of most people will grow cold.

That love is now so chilled, that also in the Netherlands millions apparently don't care that not only their own future, but also that of their own children is sacrificed on the humanity-shattering altar that was erected for the geopolitical lust for power of the unscrupulous US/EU/NATO/WeF globalists.

Declare war on Russia! Take everything from Russians! Hurt Putin by cutting off our energy and making it unaffordable! Give us that food crisis! Take away our freedoms with QR IDs and more coercive measures! Inject us all with mRNA gene manipulation injections that has already cost millions their health (or life)! Ban anyone who disagrees with the government from society! Rarely before in history has the term "death cult" been so appropriate.

But it's exactly the same in Russia, give any criticism on the governments acting and you'll go to a death camp to work until your dead, happened to millions over the reign of communism and still happens to antiwar protesters.

 So both sides are as evil as possible, it's either an technocratic death cult or an autocratic death cult. And the middle ground is peaceful living without interference from a retarded government.

The next world war in 2023?

Russian Foreign Minister Lavrov: 'Total war has been declared on us' - *End year of the complete timeline given to the prophet Daniel: 2023 (= prepare for the destruction of Europe, IF you still rise en masse)*

Now that U.S. President Joe Biden has truly violated all political and diplomatic standards of decency with seven-mile boots by scandalously calling his Russian counterpart Vladimir Putin a "murderer" (lett. butcher) who "cannot remain in power," he has sealed the fate of humanity and the planned Third World War in 2023 can no longer be prevented. Therefore, prepare yourself for the destruction of Europe - UNTIL you take massive action, not only by holding the current rulers accountable, but also by shutting off your consciousness from all daily hate-and-fear indoctrination, and recognizing that an inky black enemy is now making a final attempt to prevent humanity - and thus you! - from undergoing its possibly already very imminent promised redemption and enlightenment.

The stakes are really high now, for all of us - no one excepted. You may look around you, see the sun shining again and life seemingly going on normally.

Enjoy it, but realize that this is the most deceptive calm before the storm in history ever, and what is about to happen next will really overthrow anything you think you can still derive any security or safety from.

'Fighting for freedom'?

Biden tweeted that "we are once again in a great fight for freedom, a fight between democracy and autocracy, between freedom and oppression. This fight will not be won in days or weeks. We must harden ourselves for an upcoming long battle.'

This was in fact nothing less than an announcement of World War III, uttered according to the Alinsky method now used daily in the West: continually accuse your enemy of the very thing you yourself are most guilty of. Because freedom - where is it when you only get obligatory digital access codes if you keep getting injected with life-threatening mRNA gene manipulation injections? And "democracy"? Surely we haven't had that for a long time, neither in the US, nor in Europe, nor in the Netherlands?

Decisions in the West are made by elites, not by the people

After all, when have you ever had any say about the coming deliberately provoked war with Russia (or any previous war for that matter)? Or rather about the Covid lockdowns, vaccinations, QR codes, the authoritarian European superstate in formation, the impending transfer of our sovereignty and self-determination over your own body to the WHO (=Bill Gates), or the degradation of our affordable energy supply under the guise of a non-existent carbon climate crisis, to name just a few glaring issues?

The decisions in Washington, Moscow, Brussels and The Hague, among others, are made by the elite - not by the people, in any country. Western democracies and republics therefore differ in almost nothing from the totalitarian dictatorships they claim to be fighting. Indeed, in more and more situations - such as with the upcoming mandatory European digital QR-ID vaxpas - they are actually proving themselves to be even harsher and more inhumane, an extremely worrying and also frightening trend, which in the coming months and years threatens to crush everything built up after the last world war. (For example, there is a German bill that provides for the administration of Covid 'vaccinations' by force if necessary.)

'End of Western civilization as we know it'

Again: 'a struggle between democracy and autocracy' ? President Putin, of all people, reasonably demands free elections for the inhabitants of the Donbass, but these are - despite the Minsk agreements - flatly refused by the Ukrainian neo-Nazi fascist Zelensky, the new darling of the Western establishment (until he, too, has done his job and is pushed aside like old garbage). Not to mention the covert CIA-FBI 'coup' that brought Biden himself to power.

This is the end of Western civilization as we know it,' observes the American top economist Martin Armstrong. His A.I. Socrates once again gets it right. 'Every step Biden takes brings us to the end of the

West... The period after 2024 to 2032 will be the very worst, but for now the computer points to 2023 as the beginning of gross global violence. This is not what the world voted for.' (1)

Sanctions destroy world economy

The same is true of the rock-hard racist sanctions against Russia and Russian citizens, which are undeniably destroying the global economy. Last Friday, Foreign Minister Sergey Lavrov declared that "today a purebred hybrid war, a 'total war,' has been declared to us. This term, which was used by Hitler Germany, is now used by many European politicians when they talk about what they want to do with Russia. Their objectives are not hidden, but are announced publicly: they want to destroy, devastate, ruin and suffocate the Russian economy and Russia as a whole.' (4)

Even Switzerland is now following the Czech Republic in confiscating all property of Russians in the country, a measure thus based solely on someone's ethnicity - exactly as was done in the US during WW-2, when everything was taken from Japanese citizens in the US and they were eventually put in camps. (Who again claimed that we have learned something from history? Now where is the "Russian Lives Matter" movement?)

As a result of these sanctions, Western capital is withdrawing not only unprecedentedly massively from Russia, but also from China and all other emerging economies (2). These capital flows historically always precede a major war. Moreover, Biden has threatened to hit China with similarly harsh sanctions.

Therefore, the leaders in Beijing realize that they are next on the list who will have to choose between bowing and groveling to the US /EU/ NATO/ WEF/ WHO/ IMF dominated New World Order, or being attacked and subjugated both economically and militarily, or even being destroyed.

No other option but 'total war against tyrannical West'?

The Western globalists are clearly out for regime change in Moscow, but it's not going to happen. On the contrary, because of the insane Russophobia in America and Europe, the Russian people are aligning themselves even more strongly with President Putin. It has also driven Russia even faster into the arms of China.

Both countries, which recently signed a strong defense pact, realize that there is probably no other option left but to jointly wage an all-out war against the tyrannical West, as long as it is still dominated by the U.S. and the World Economic Forum of Klaus 'Great Reset' Schwab, whose 'Build Back Better' agenda requires the destruction of the current energy and food system, as well as a sharp reduction in the world's population by billions.

Armstrong: 'It pains me to write this, but people who understand know where this is going: World War III.

59

And make no mistake: this is being done intentionally!'
NATO Secretary General Jens Stoltenberg also
demanded at a press conference on March 24 that
'China must not provide economic or military support to
Russia.' A day earlier, he had even accused Beijing of
spreading "blatant lies and misinformation.

As is well known, misinformation/disinformation today
is EVERYTHING that goes against the prescribed
narrative of the Western establishment - i.e., against
the propaganda of Washington, Brussels and Davos.

Zelensky at Oscars to promote WW3?

Zelensky may be brought on stage at the Oscar
ceremony to sell "his" World War III. No one will point
out to him that he could have also very easily complied
with the Minsk Accords, and met Putin's very
reasonable demands. Then the current Russian
operation in Ukraine would never have been necessary,
and we would not now be saddled with the risk of
another major world conflagration.

But the West is sure to cheer and clap again for this
'former' comedian and self-proclaimed Russophobe.
'Don't worry, you'll get your way,' Armstrong responds
cynically. 'World War III is coming, and 2023 is not going
to be a fun story. Biden may say that no one needs to
fear nuclear war, but he himself is using the Doomsday-
747. Terrible to have to write this, but unless people call
their representatives of the people on this, you had
better consider emigrating to the South.'

Daniel and 2023

From a spiritual standpoint, there are some notable prophetic indications that the years 2023 and 2024 could become crucial. Note that these are not certain 'predictions', of course, but given world events, some striking chronologies are nevertheless apparent.

In 2014, in the article "First of 4 blood moons - prophetic or coincidence?", I first mentioned the possible importance of the year 2023: The '1260' days in Revelation are a repeat of the '1260' prophetic days (=years) as revealed to the Old Testament prophet Daniel. Daniel was shown by an angel the future of 'your people' (the Israelites) (9:24, 10:14, 11:14, 12:1). (A period of 2 x 1260 = 2520 years, plus an end time of 75 years).

The first period ended with the construction of the Islamic Dome of the Rock (the "abomination of desolation") in Temple Square. What is special is that after the second period of 1260 years (in the 'desert' = the dispersion over the Earth) two short periods of 30 and 45 years respectively are mentioned, or an end time that lasts a total of 75 years: 'Blessed is he who continues to expect and reaches 1335 days' (= reaches the 1335th year).

Converted into day-years, this period ends in 2023. Calculated from the second set of prophecies given to Daniel 19 years later, 2042 was also initially a possibility. Given the acceleration of time (lines), however, it seems clear that it cannot last that long anymore, and it will indeed be 2023 (/2024) (or some years thereafter).

(2023, by the way, is also the target year of Turkish President Erdogan to begin the re-establishment of the Ottoman Empire, which at the time also held parts of Europe and tried several times to conquer our entire continent).

Abraham and 2024

A parallel can also be drawn between Archfather Abraham and the year 2024. Archfather Terah was born in the year 1878 from Adam. 70 years later, his son Abraham was born. Abraham was 75 years old when he left Haran, which corresponds to the year 2023.

After traveling some 800 kilometers, he arrived in the Promised Land, but there was a famine there, so he had to travel on to Egypt. After some time he returned, after which in Bethel there is the well-known 'separation' from Lot. We know that he was 76 at the time, because it is written that Abraham lived in the land for 10 years and was 86 years old when Ishmael was born (Genesis 16:16).

So Abraham finally arrived in the promised land in the year 2024 (from Adam). While it is a very indirect connection, could this - given the enormous significance of Abraham to all of human history - mean that a new 'arrival' in the 'promised land' will follow in 2024 (a New Earth perhaps?) for those who have prepared themselves for it in their minds and consciousness? (See also: 'The Great Awakening will only come as soon as humanity is in danger of being exterminated')

A nuclear threat?

Largest gas field Gazprom in Europe LEAKS: 2 weeks at most and hundreds of millions will go cold - *Romania distributes 30 million anti-radiation pills to population*

(04.00) - Russian politician Alexei Zhuravlyov, chairman of the centrist Rodina party, has threatened on a state radio station to launch a nuclear attack on Warsaw and NATO troops who dare to cross the border with Ukraine supposedly for a "peace mission". NATO Secretary General Jens Stoltenberg stated that the use of nuclear weapons will change the conflict, and that Russia "can never win a nuclear war. This is true, but Russia can survive such a nuclear conflict much better because it can hide and protect 45 million civilians underground. There are hardly any such hiding places in NATO countries.

Moreover, the alliance is trying to cover up with this kind of tough talk that in reality it is terrified by the combination of Russian hypersonic missiles and highly advanced missile defense systems capable of intercepting Western nuclear missiles

Stoltenberg, however, stoically asserted that NATO has plans ready to protect all allies from a nuclear threat, and that no one should doubt that the alliance is prepared for anything. In Romania, they are taking this very literally by handing out 30 million potassium iodide pills to the population - a hardly sensible measure, by the way, since they do not help against other forms of radioactive radiation and fallout. Despite this, a run on these pills has also begun in Belgium and Norway.

'Direct collision' between NATO and Russia near?

Russia's foreign minister warned of a 'direct clash' between Russia and NATO if a 'peacekeeping force' is stationed in Ukraine. 'Our Polish colleagues have already said that there will be a NATO summit and peacekeepers should be sent. I hope they understand what is at stake.'

Meanwhile, there is increasingly serious talk in the U.S. about a "no-fly" zone over Ukraine. If this were to be enforced by, for example, the US aircraft carrier USS Truman sailing in the Mediterranean, a direct military confrontation with Russia would follow and World War III would be a fact.

Gas almost gone, Europe commits suicide

In the West, people still seem to think that President Putin will not dare to press the 'red button'. That is why they are still doing everything they can to destroy Russia financially and economically with outrageous discrimination and sanctions that are as unjust as they are absurd. This will not really succeed, because if Europe wants to keep warm and continue to receive Russian gas, it will have to pay for it in rubles from now on. This means that the Russian central bank will be able to replenish its depleted foreign currency reserves.

If the EU continues to refuse, our gas supply will soon
be finished, especially since gas prices have risen by
another 20% after the Kremlin's decision. In fact,
Gazprom's largest European gas storage field in
Germany (UGS Rehden) is LEEG. Another 10, 14 days or
so and hundreds of millions of Europeans could be very
cold, and/or unable to cook.

Moreover, the credibility of the euro and the dollar is
now definitively "destroyed," as Putin put it bluntly. It is
in fact Russia which is rich in raw materials and natural
resources (and which also wants to exploit them), and
especially Europe which has virtually NOTHING. And
what it has, such as natural gas, it refuses to use any
longer.

Some NATO countries literally want 'Ukrainians to keep fighting and dying' to prevent Russia from achieving any political victory - *Upcoming NATO membership Finland 'provocation that will lead to nuclear war'*

Le Figaro, the oldest French newspaper, is reporting, based on information from a source in French intelligence, that U.S. Delta Force and British SAS elite units are waging a "secret war" in Ukraine against the Russian military. This would mean that Western and Russian forces - despite denials from Washington and London - are directly fighting each other, thus justifying the conclusion that World War III has actually unofficially begun.

SAS units "have been present in Ukraine since the beginning of the war, as have the U.S. Deltas," tweeted Le Figaro's senior international correspondent Georges Malbrunot based on his source. The special forces are said to be actively fighting the Russian army.

British Prime Minister Boris Johnson is one of the biggest supporters of the fascist neo-Nazi regime in Kiev, and is said to have personally urged President Zelensky to keep fighting the Russians, and not to make peace until better terms are offered. Zelensky has since announced large-scale war operations in the east and south, and said that his army is dependent on U.S. arms supplies in doing so.

Earlier, the Daily Mirror wrote that "former" SAS soldiers were allegedly engaged by an unnamed European country through a private company in Ukraine for reconnaissance and anti-tank warfare. The Kremlin therefore invariably talks about 'mercenaries' fighting on the side of Ukraine.

Statements EU and NATO increasingly bellicose

Josep Borell, senior EU representative for foreign affairs, said last Saturday on a visit to Kiev that "the war will be won on the battlefield. In doing so, Brussels also indicated it was not interested in peace with Russia. Borell promised another €500 million and new arms supplies to Ukraine. Russian Foreign Minister Lavrov responded that Russia "will never give in to pressure," and that Borell's "extraordinary" statement on the war "significantly changes the rules of the game.

Meanwhile, the Americans have more than 100,000 troops stationed in Europe. The Washington Post explicitly reported that "it is better for some in NATO, which may be expanded to include Sweden and Finland as early as a few months from now, that the Ukrainians continue to fight and die, rather than bring about peace that either comes too soon, or at too high a price for Kiev and the rest of Europe.

Indeed, a number of NATO countries would not give Russian President Putin even "the semblance of a victory. A Ukrainian peace activist therefore accused the

US of using his country only 'as cannon fodder' against Russia. 'The U.S. government supported two coups in Ukraine in 10 years, spurring a war that has cost 14,000 Ukrainians their lives.'

Russians pump water into steel plant to force neo-Nazis out

According to the Russian Defense Ministry, Ukraine unsuccessfully tried to use a passenger ship to evacuate leaders of the ultranationalist (neo-Nazi) Azov battalion and foreign mercenaries from Mariupol. Hundreds of mercenaries and thousands of Azov fighters are said to be trapped in the city as a result. The 36th Marine Brigade put a 'goodbye' on their Facebook page this morning, as they are almost out of ammunition. 'Following this will be man-to-man fighting. Further for some death, and for some captivity.'

In the catacombs of the important Azovstal steel plant in the south of Mariupol, some 3,000 neo-Nazis of the Azov regiment are said to be hiding, as well as possibly NATO officers, who, according to as yet unconfirmed reports, are said to be working for a secret biolab located there. They may not be able to hide for much longer, as the Russians have ordered fire trucks to pump the underground chambers full of water, so that everyone will be forced to come out.

Last Friday, a Ukrainian Tochka-U missile exploded at the Kramatorsk train station, killing 50 people. Western media and politicians naturally immediately blamed

Russia, but the Tochka-U missile has not been in use by the Russian military for years. It is clear that the Ukrainian army wanted to use the fleeing civilians as human shields.

'NATO membership Finland will lead to nuclear war'

Institute for Political Economy front man Paul Craig Roberts, former member of the Reagan administration, writes that Finland's possible upcoming NATO membership will be perceived by the Kremlin as a provocation for the same reason as a Ukrainian membership: because it will allow the Western alliance to deploy missiles that can hit Moscow within minutes.

Vladimir Dzhabarov, a member of the Russian Federation Council, openly threatened that Finland "will become a target" if it becomes a NATO member. 'I think it would be a terrible tragedy for the whole Finnish people', one that will end in 'the destruction of their country'.

Roberts: 'I have been emphasizing for years that these provocations against Russia will eventually cross a red line and end in nuclear war. I have also long been critical of the Kremlin for not stopping these provocations by responding in a forceful manner.' According to Roberts, Putin should have conquered Ukraine with brute force in a matter of days, which would have immediately sent a message to the West that countries that support U.S./NATO aggression will not fare well.

Since nothing is published in the Western mainstream media anymore that deviates from the Pentagon and NATO propaganda narrative, 'nothing can be done about this insane drive toward nuclear war,' Roberts believes. 'Once again the world is sleepwalking toward war. But this war will be nuclear and the last war.'

Another war in the east?

Is Israel taking action before Russian missiles are deployed in Iran? - *Israel and Iran play major roles in each other's end time prophecies - Is the true Man and Messiah being sidelined with a false end time scenario?*

On the backdrop of the war in Ukraine and its many far-reaching effects on energy, fuel and food prices, a crucial line was crossed on March 31 in the long-standing conflict between Israel (/ Saudi Arabia) and Iran. The U.S. Ambassador to Israel, Tom Nides. stated last Thursday, March 31, that Israel will no longer face any blockade from the U.S. if the decision is made to attack Iran, even if a new nuclear deal with the Islamic Republic is unexpectedly reached. Previous imminent Israeli attacks on Iran were always blocked by Washington. Now that this is no longer the case, a new war, with probably even more serious consequences for the world than the conflict in Ukraine, seems only a matter of time.

Threats of war back and forth for some 15 years

For some 15 years we have been hearing from Jerusalem that it will be "only a few months" before Iran has a nuclear bomb, and Israel is therefore on the verge of destroying the country's nuclear facilities. Indeed, the mullahs in Tehran have openly vowed numerous times to totally destroy the 'Zionist regime'; a risk little Israel, which has no defensive buffer spatially, cannot afford to take.

That Iranian nuclear bomb - as far as we know - is still not there, but nevertheless the same warnings and threats keep being repeated over and over again. At a certain point, that constant yelling back and forth was taken seriously by few anymore. That does not mean, however, that the danger of such an attack has diminished.

Quite the contrary, in fact. Now that the world has turned its attention to other pressing matters, and the West conveniently assumes that a new (or restored) nuke deal (JCPOA) with Iran is on the way, the Israelis could decide to take advantage of the situation by striking unexpectedly, especially now that the biggest hurdle of all, the American veto (which was kept intact even under Donald Trump), has been removed for the first time in all those years.

'Israel's hands are not (no longer) tied'

Last Thursday, the U.S. ambassador to Israel, Tom Nides, told Channel 12 that the U.S. 'does not expect Israel to sit still and do nothing at all' if a final deal is reached with Iran. 'We have been very clear about this. If we have a deal, then Israel's hands are not tied. And if we don't have a deal, then Israel's hands are certainly not tied. Israel can take all kinds of actions that are necessary to protect the state of Israel.

Nides continued that President Joe Biden - who could go on to add three more (Russia directly, China, Iran) to the one new war he started (Ukraine) - is 'doing everything he can to make sure Iran doesn't get a nuclear weapon.

Iran has little reason to cooperate anymore

Since the U.S. withdrawal from the JCPOA in 2018, Washington has reinstated all previous sanctions against Iran. As a result, Tehran has also withdrawn several agreements, including a promised limit on enriching uranium and testing new ballistic missiles that could theoretically carry nuclear weapons.

Iran was initially willing to curb its nuclear technology development, but demanded guarantees that it would not be subjected to an invasion like Iraq, or be bombed to pieces like Libya, or be overrun like Syria by a terrorist army (ISIS) trained and armed by the CIA and Turkish intelligence.

But now that Israel has been given the green light to attack Iran regardless of any deal at its discretion, the only remaining reason for Tehran not to build a nuclear bomb effectively falls away. After all, the strict Western sanctions against the country - which, by the way, are being evaded with the help of China and Russia - are still intact. (1)

Refugees from Ukraine and a summit in the Negev

By mid-March, some 200,000 refugees from Ukraine had already arrived in Israel. The city of Jerusalem is expecting another 10,000, mostly Jews, this week (2). Whether Israel will thus already plunge into a highly uncertain military adventure against Iran in the near future remains to be seen, given the reception of so many new people.

Last Sunday, in the Sde Boker kibbutz in the Negev, there was a unique summit between ministers and diplomats from Israel, the US, the United Arab Emirates, Bahrain, Morocco and Egypt. Saudi Arabia was also invited, but stayed away in protest at the U.S. intention to strike a new nuclear deal with Iran. The Saudis are also angry that President Biden will no longer provide arms for the proxy war being waged in Yemen with Iranian-backed Houthi rebels, who have managed to shell and damage Saudi oil facilities in Jeddah and elsewhere.

Will Israel take action before Russian missiles are deployed in Iran?

Israel, as a small country, is afraid that a handful of Iranian nuclear bombs will totally destroy it. On the other hand, the Israelis possess at least 80, but according to other sources an estimated 200 to 300 nuclear weapons, some of which are placed on submarines. Israel is therefore always in a position to retaliate maximally against an attack, and completely incinerate Iran. This Tehran will no doubt be aware of. It is partly for this reason that that war between the two countries that has been announced so many times in 12 to 15 years has still not happened.

According to an unconfirmed report in March, the Kremlin is said to have stated that "Iran will play a crucial role in the Russian nuclear deterrent. If true, this would be a downright 'game changer' that would make an Israeli attack impossible in the future. Jerusalem may therefore feel compelled to take action in the near future.

Should Israel indeed proceed with a direct military attack on Iran's nuclear facilities, that operation - for which it earmarked $900 million over a year ago - will most likely set in motion a much larger international war in the Middle East that will presumably also involve the U.S., NATO, Russia and possibly China. If the war in Ukraine is still going on at that time, then one could justifiably speak of the beginning of World War III.

Israel and Iran play major roles in each other's end-time prophecies

Shi'ite Muslims (mainly living in Iran and Iraq) believe that in the end times the 12th Imam will return together with Isa (the Islamic version of Jesus) to defeat Israel and the West, and impose Islam as the only true religion on humanity worldwide.

Jews in Israel and Christians worldwide see Iran precisely as a core part of the Gog-out-Magog coalition (Ezekiel 38) that will attack Israel. This coalition consists of Magog, Persia (Iran), Cush (Sudan), Put (Libya), Lydia (Western Turkey) Gomer and Beth-Togarma (Turkey).

Magog is almost always interpreted as Russia, but every serious classical Bible encyclopedia and atlas tells us that Magog was not in present-day Russia. Both Magog, Mesek, Tubal, Gomer and Beth-Togarma were in Asia Minor, to be precise the Muslim republics south of Russia (including Turkey, Uzbekistan, Kazakhstan, Turkmenistan, Azerbaijan).

The prophet Zechariah describes how Israel will parry this massive Islamic attack from all sides (better known as "Armageddon" (also described by the prophet Joel), although some interpreters think this is yet another war) with nuclear weapons, destroying all participants in this coalition.

A Third Temple?

Before that happens, especially evangelical and Pentecostal Christians expect a peace treaty with Israel, after which the Third Temple would be built. Preparations for its construction have been going on for decades; for example, numerous gold objects (such as the Menorah) and also priestly robes have been ready for quite some time, as has the 'first stone'.

Orthodox Jewish groups in particular expect that their Messiah will build this Temple - which may be a "gateway" to another, dark dimension - and rule the world from there. On the contrary, the Christian groups mentioned above think that this figure is "the Antichrist," who will begin a horrific persecution against the remaining Christians, and then also wage wars to subjugate the world to himself.

Is the true Man and Messiah being sidelined with a false scenario?

The position of Israel is by no means uncontroversial in both Judaism and Christianity. This is partly due to the fact that the infamous Rothschild family (the satanic "Pharisee" bloodline) had a big hand in the creation of the Jewish state and still has a lot of influence. According to some, the present-day Israel is therefore a "fake" Jewish state designed solely to stage "Armageddon" and the coming of a false Messiah, as a kind of self-fulfilling prophecy.

Although there are still numerous uncertainties, Israel's policies and behavior, especially in recent years, seem to indicate that the little country is indeed only being used as a kind of 'vassal state' of Freemasonry to deliberately carry out a (false) religious end-time scenario, which is to convince Christians, Jews and Muslims alike that the Apocalypse has occurred and the true Messiah has returned to establish the 1000 year kingdom of peace on Earth.

However, it is certainly not inconceivable that this very scenario is a monstrous Luciferian deception to bind mankind forever to that "real" false Christ, the real "antichrist" who will "completely sideline the True Man and Messiah".

Biodigital Convergence: Governments actively working toward full integration human with digital entities

The now infamous futurist and WEF speaker Yuval Noah Harari, professor of history at the Hebrew University of Jerusalem and top advisor to Klaus Schwab, is winding down and acknowledging that Covid-19 is being used to put everyone "under the skin under total biometric surveillance. This means that the mandatory introduction of implanted/injected nanochips is now well and truly upon us, and the digital aspect of the 'Mark of the Beast' will be a fait accompli within a few years. We suspect that many vaccinated people, whose bodies have already been injected with mRNA nanotech via the Covid 'vaccines', have by now been brainwashed to such an extent that they will eagerly queue up for that chip. Fine, they'll know right away if I'm infected!"

Covid is crucial, because it convinces people to accept and acknowledge total biometric control. If we want to stop this epidemic, we have to monitor not just people, but what's going on under their skin.' 'That's what governments want to know: what's our body temperature? Our blood pressure? Our medical condition (or vaccination status)?'

Some of Harari's well-known earlier statements:

In an interview with 60 Minutes, he once said that 'so far we've seen companies and governments collecting data on where we go, who we meet, and what movies we watch. In the next phase, control will go under our skin.'

'People are gaining greater power than ever. We develop actual divine powers of creation and destruction. We upgrade humans to gods, and gain the power to redesign life.... Humans are now hackable animals (CNN inverview November 2019). The whole idea that people have a soul or spirit, that they have free will and nobody knows what's going on inside them, that they have free will to make a choice, whether it's for the election or at the supermarket, is over.'

'Data is worth much more in the world today than money. Ten years ago, big companies were paying billions for WhatsApp and In-stagram, and people wondered if they were crazy. The reason? Because they were producing data. Increasingly, the world is being more or less split into spheres of data collection and collation. In the Cold War, you had the Iron Curtain. Now we have the Silicon Curtain between the US and China: where does the data go? California, or to Shenzhen, Shanghai and Beijing?'

Biodigital convergence

In 2020, Policy Horizons, a strategic organization within Canadian government, published the report 'Exploring

Biodigital Convergence', which stated that already in the near future 'biology and digital technology' will merge, and a new kind of (transhuman) human will emerge. On that subject, once 'science fiction' but now becoming reality, we have written extensively in recent years.

'It is more than a technological change. This biodigital convergence (fusion) may transform the way we understand ourselves, and cause us to redefine what we consider human or natural... Digital technologies and biological systems are beginning to unite and merge with each other in ways that may deeply disrupt our assumptions about society, the economy and our bodies. We call this the biodigital convergence. Which opens up amazing new ways to change human beings - our bodies, minds and behaviors... (And) to change or create other organisms.'

For those who still don't want to believe what was and/or may have been put into the Covid-19 injections, 'Digital technology can be embedded in organisms, and biological components can exist as parts of digital technologies. The physical mixing, manipulation, and confluence of the biological and the digital create new hybrid life forms and new technology, each functioning with often enhanced capabilities in the tangible world.'

Brain interfaces and neural implants

For example, robots with biological brains and biological bodies with digital brains already exist, as do human-computer and brain-machine interfaces. Digitally manipulated insects such as drone dragonflies and "surveillance" grasshoppers are examples of this merging of bio with digi-tech. By tapping into our nervous system, neurons can be manipulated, and tech can be added to change the function and purpose of an organism. For example, scientists have already equipped rat brains with many additional "wires" that can be used to deliver information and commands to the brain.

Humans are given digital interfaces in (/ to) their brains, with which they can give thought commands to, for example, open an app that, via injected nanotech, monitors and, if necessary, adjusts the health of the body.

In this way, contact could also be made with the Internet, which will then have evolved into the Metaverse (/Metaversum), to which in time many will presumably remain almost chronically linked. The interface also records your dreams, allowing you to look back and analyze them later. It also allows you to program your dreams.

In short: the classical concept of what 'life' is, will in fact disappear. Life will no longer be purely biological, but also - and in the long run perhaps especially and even totally - technological. For some this may sound fantastic, but don't forget that neural and other physical implants and (nano)tech will be under constant external A.I. 5G/6G control, and you really won't have any freedom or privacy anymore, so also - as Harari said - you won't have any freedom of choice or free will.

Most people happy with android slave status

People will even be able to be programmed to be perfectly happy with their android slave status. Any memory of what it was once like to be a natural, free and independent human being will be stopped and erased. Personally, it seems to me an abomination of the worst order, but for many people who actually find life too difficult and complicated, handing over all responsibilities may be music to their ears.

When I look at how thoughtlessly and mindlessly the vast majority of the population agreed to the most absurd and pernicious corona measures from 2020 onwards, and then to now highly harmful experimental mRNA gene manipulation injections, I fear that this may well be true for the vast majority. And that, of course, is exactly what the WEF elite are all about ("You'll own nothing and be happy").

WEF announced digital 'sign of the Beast' almost literally in February

On February 20, we paid attention to the new WEF report Advancing Towards Digital Agency, which almost literally announced a digital 'sign of the Beast' system. The bottom line is that everyone is going to have some kind of personal digital 'god' who is going to make all the important decisions for you, because based on all your personal data, that 'god' would know exactly what you want and need, and when and where. And 'of course' the government is going to totally control ANY aspect of this process, this 'god', and therefore YOU.

This digital profile 'may contain inherent data characteristics (such as biometrics)(= physical characteristics), or assigned characteristics (such as names or national ID numbers)'. Once this digital ID, which will be embedded in your body in the next phase, is in place and embedded, it will also include your purchasing behavior and medical situation, plus your 'assessments and decisions' based on your profile and social/financial behavior ('a bank decides the attractiveness of an individual for a loan'). This is nothing less than the social credit system as rolled out in China.

Integrating transhuman humans with global control system

The use of (eventually mandatory) 'vaccinations' with advanced (nano) tech to build the 'sign of the Beast' system IN your body, so that you will surrender your free will in ALL areas and will no longer be able to resist this A.I. 'god' in the making, we predicted back in 2009. (See also our article of 03-09: 'Implantable 5G nanotech biosensor already as of 2021 in Covid-19 vaccines' (/ Transhuman being integrated with global digital control system)).

There will be no escape from that system, not only because it is deliberately designed as a kind of eternal prison and because these gene therapy injections will have irreversible health consequences for many anyway, but also because you will become an inseparable part of that technocratic 'Beast' system, in which you will be 'online' every second of the day to follow, control, steer, modify and change.

Just as you cannot remove the mRNA nanotech and spikes of the Covid 'vaccines' from your body, you will find it impossible to remove yourself from 'the Beast' because you have 'fused' with it. Indeed, you will no longer be an original 'human', but will have been transformed into a transhuman android, a kind of 'cyborg'.

Then you will be worshipped by a digital 'god' forever, a cyborg god: the A.I. of Schwab's 'Internet of Bodies', the digital personification of Lucifer (/ Satan) on Earth.

The big C is still a threat?

Pfizer document acknowledged as early as last year existence of 'Covid vaccine shedding' that via skin-to-skin contact and 'breathing the same air' leads to disruption of menstruation and even miscarriages

Dr. Philippe van Welbergen, medical director of Biomedical Clinics, has shown, based on blood samples from both vaccinated and unvaccinated people, that the graphene oxide injected into people via Covid injections organizes itself in the body and builds up into larger, more complex structures and wires. The graphene oxide also acquires magnetic properties and/or an electrical charge.

Also, according to him, 'shards' of graphene oxide would be transferred from vaccinated to unvaccinated people, with the latter also suffering from blood clots and destroyed blood cells.

Van Welbergen was one of the first to warn the public with photos of blood samples in 2021 about the damage the Covid injections do to human blood cells. His patients last year began complaining of chronic fatigue, dizziness, memory problems, menstrual disorders, and sometimes even paralysis. In the blood of the vaxxers, he found unusual tube-like structures of graphene, some particles of which lit up. Lots of blood cells were damaged; few healthy cells remained.

Blood samples show severe damage from 'vaccines'

In February, during a Loving Life TV livestream, he showed footage from his most recent study of more than 100 blood samples from both vaccinated and unvaccinated people. He showed that that the unvaccinated were "infected with vaccine toxins by shedding.

Compare the following two image with each other. The first is a shot of healthy blood cells; the second is of someone who has been injected with a Covid 'vaccine'. Graft threads and all kinds of clots can clearly be seen. One of the very few healthy blood cells can still be seen in the circle. The hollow graphene threads contain red blood cells, and will start blocking capillaries.

'Dr. Philippe', as he is called, additionally discovered a magnetic or electrical polarity effect on different sides of these graphene threads. In the image below, you can see a strange 'C' like opening that wasn't there before, which he says is an indication that the reaction of the vaccine substances with the surrounding blood cells has changed. 'And I don't know what triggered this.'

Below is a blood sample from an unvaccinated three-year-old child, which contains "shards" of graphene resulting from shedding. In other words, the graphene oxide has been transferred from the vaccinated parents to the unvaccinated child.

The following image shows the blood of an 8-year-old unvaccinated child, whose blood has been contaminated and destroyed by the transfer of graphene by vaccinated people in her environment. The girl's right arm and upper right leg are effectively paralyzed. The child can no longer lift his or her arm, and the femur no longer functions properly.

Health hazard from contact with vaccinated persons alone

Little attention has been paid so far to Dr. Philippes findings and presentation, which is surprising, since the consequences are very far-reaching and serious. If other scientists support his conclusions, it means that not only are the health and lives of Covid vaxxers at great risk, but also the unvaccinated should be very careful about frequent contact with vaccinated people, especially in places where many people are together.

A frequently reported side effect of the Covid mRNA injections in women and girls is irregular or otherwise disrupted menstruation. Thousands of women have now suffered miscarriages, and several newborn babies have died.

Hundreds of unvaccinated women have prepared statements saying they have had the same symptoms and miscarriages just from having contact with vaccinated people.

A Pfizer document, in note, confirms that these serious effects may indeed be the result of vaccine-shedding:

Dr. Naomi Wolf posted hundreds of these testimonials from both vaccinated and unvaccinated women on Facebook in April, but they were quickly blocked:

ABC7 News reporter Kate Larsen asked on social media in the same month if any women experienced these types of symptoms after being injected. She received many thousands of replies from concerned women who complained of (often severe) bleeding that sometimes lasted for weeks, or in whom menstruation actually disappeared. There were also women who after the transition suddenly started menstruating again, which according to holistic medicine is a signal of cancer. (See also: 11-01-21: mRNA vaccines: genetic engineering is dangerous because it can cause infertility).

In the US alone, more than 4,000 women have officially lost their unborn or newborn child in just 16 months. Bear in mind that these VAERS statistics historically reflect only 1% of the actual number. For comparison, since 1990, "only" 565 women have suffered the same fate after a flu vaccination, meaning that a Covid injection gives a 16633% higher chance of miscarriage. There were 2238 miscarriages recorded in 30 years as a result of ALL other approved vaccines.

Pfizer and governments knew about mRNA vaccine shedding

In the Pfizer document "A PHASE 1/2/3, PLACEBO-CONTROLLED, RANDOMIZED, OBSERVER-BLIND, DOSE-FINDING STUDY TO EVALUATE THE SAFETY,

TOLERABILITY, IMMUNOGENICITY, AND EFFICACY OF SARS-COV-2 RNA VACCINE CANDIDATES AGAINST COVID-19 IN HEALTHY INDIVIDUALS," there is an entire section on the possibility of "mRNA vaccine shedding. So Pfizer acknowledges that it is possible for you, as an unvaccinated person, to become 'infected' merely by having been in close proximity to an unvaccinated person.'

We have covered this before. On May 8, 2021, for example, we wrote: "In addition to potential permanent or fatal damage to one's own health, it appears that vaccine recipients may also pose a danger to unvaccinated people.

This is because the many corona 'wappies' who have just received their shots are turned into walking 'spike factories', and can then exhale these spike proteins. Through this process of 'shedding' they can thus infect other people.'

I myself regularly have a somewhat hoarse throat when I have been in contact with toasted people. After a maximum of a few hours these symptoms disappear again. From others I have heard complaints ranging from blurred vision, headaches, dizziness, nausea, and ear or nose bleeds.

In our article of April 29, 2021 (More and more reports of unvaccinated people getting sick after contact with vaccinated people) you can read that it is a scientifically established fact that humans exhale a large number of proteins. This could very well include the (toxic) spike protein that the Covid mRNA 'vaccine' codes for.

Nevertheless (or precisely because of that?) they forced the Covid-19 vaccines on billions of people with maximum compulsion and daily extremely misleading propaganda. Especially in the countries with the highest vaccination coverage, the serious health consequences are starting to become more and more painfully visible.

Already more than 62,000 vaccinated in EU got eye problems

WHO warns of new form of severe hepatitis in children; Pfizer study acknowledges vaccine may be cause.

7500% more cancer after start of Covid injections and 1000% more dead and sick children aged 5 to 11 (vs. all other vaccines) - Injections kill twice as many blacks and Latinos as whites

While Denmark has suspended the Covid-19 'vaccinations' at least until after the summer now that 81% of the population has received two doses and 61.6% a booster shot, and there are hardly any people left in the hospital (which, by the way, is perfectly normal for spring), for some time now we have been hearing from various quarters about (often young) people who have had vision problems after a Covid injection.

Now blindness is one of the many potentially serious side effects of the injections from Pfizer, Moderna, AstraZeneca and J&J.

Statistics show that the number of vaccinated people who begin to see poorly or even go completely blind is increasing weekly. According to a fact sheet from the Stroke Foundation in Australia, approximately one-third of brain hemorrhage survivors experience permanent blindness (partial or otherwise). Brain hemorrhages are one of the other dangerous side effects of the Covid vaccines.

More than 62,000 Europeans with eye problems

Over a week ago, the number of Europeans who have suffered eye problems as a result of the Pfizer 'vaccine' already stood at 30,574 (including 47 deaths). Moderna caused 8993 eye disorders (including 35 deaths), AstraZeneca 20,999 (including 34 deaths), Janssen (J&J) 1914 (including 12 deaths) and Novavax 13. In total, therefore, 62,493 people in the EU already suffered a harvest disorder, of whom 128 did not survive. Please note that these are the official figures from EudraVigilance, the adverse drug reactions database of the European Medicines Agency in Amsterdam, which, according to extensive university research, on average reflects only 6% of the actual number of cases and victims.

The same picture is visible in Great Britain: almost 25,000 people with eye problems after a Covid injection, 531 of whom have gone completely blind.

In addition, there are dozens of other people who became (partially) blind in one eye, have prolonged or permanent blurred vision, or are suddenly unable to see for a few seconds or minutes at unexpected times.

Mainstream media and 'fact checkers' invariably claim that these cases are not necessarily caused by a Covid 'vaccine'. They forget to mention that there are lots of reports of people who developed eye problems shortly after their injection(s). Take Louis for example, whose wife went completely blind in her left eye 4 days after her AstraZeneca shot, and 30%-60% blind in her right eye. Almost everyone now realizes that this cannot possibly be a "coincidence.

Cerebral hemorrhages cause blindness

Brain hemorrhages are another known dangerous side effect. In the UK alone, there are 3141 cases and 235 deaths due to Pfizer and AstraZeneca injections. The Stroke Foundation in Australia reports in a fact sheet that about one-third of brain hemorrhage survivors suffer permanent vision loss. Most do not regain (full) vision.

The reason brain hemorrhages cause blindness is that the nerves of each eye are connected to the brain together, so usually both eyes are damaged by a brain hemorrhage.

This can occur because it has been proven that the nanotech particles in the injections penetrate all parts of the brain, and also create the toxic spikes, which the "vaccines" the body codes for, in the brain. The body then attacks these spikes, and thus its own brain.

New form of severe hepatitis in children

The Covid injections have been wreaking havoc on the health of millions of recipients since the beginning of 2021. A few days ago, the WHO issued a warning about a new form of severe hepatitis in 74 children so far, which has been found in Great Britain, Spain and Ireland, among other countries.

Pfizer has confirmed in its own studies that the spike proteins do indeed travel throughout the body and do not remain at the injection site, as was claimed last year. The highest concentration of spikes appears to accumulate in the liver, and in addition in the spleen, adrenal glands and ovaries.

Scientists at Lund University even discovered that the Pfizer mRNA "vaccine" can be incorporated into the DNA of liver cells. They also found spikes on the surface of liver cells that can be attacked by the immune system, causing autoimmune hepatitis.

Children aged 5 to 11 must now also receive a 'booster' if it is up to Pfizer, and this is despite the fact that the first two injections in this age group caused an increase in mortality (9 deaths) and morbidity (43 permanently disabled) of more than 1000% over all other 'vaccines'.

Vaxxers then often say: oh, but those numbers are still very low. Indeed, but it will be your own (grand)child! Consider that in 2009 a few dozen deaths (all ages) were enough to stop the swine flu vaccinations.

More than 43.000 deaths in EU; explosion of cancer cases

The total number of officially counted fatalities from Covid shots in the EU on April 9 was 43,005, some 2.54% of the total number of cases. As many as 1.88 million serious adverse events were counted up to that point (45.85% of the total).

In an interview with The Vigilant Fox, Dr. Ryan Cole told us that he gets reports from all over the world from doctors who see the number of cancer patients exploding. A look at the official US VAERS statistics shows that in 16 months, 739 cases of cancer (with 84 deaths) due to the Covid 'vaccines' have been reported. In the 30 years prior to that, there were 'only' 220 cases and 16 deaths, which translates to a 7567% increase.

Last but not least: On April 8, the VAERS added over 100 miscarriages after one week that occurred after the mother took a Covid-19 vaccine. This brought the total number of miscarriages to 4023. That's far more in just 16 months than the 3134 of any other vaccine ever taken. (8)

Injections kill twice as many blacks and Latinos as whites

U.S. Health Secretary Xavier Becerra has said that "we know that vaccines are killing twice as many people of color...blacks, Latinos, Native Americans (Indians), as white Americans.

The likely reason is chronic vitamin D3 deficiency. People with darker skin are often unaware that their pigment blocks the production of vitamin D by sunlight in their skin. As of 2020, numerous studies have shown a direct link between severe Covid patients and vitamin D deficiency. People with high levels in their blood appear to get sick much less, or not at all. So this also applies to white people.

German Dr. Sucharit Bhakdi (Doctors for Covid Ethics) gained worldwide fame for being one of the first system scientists to seriously warn people not to take a Covid-19 vaccine.

He wrote the notorious bestseller "Corona False Alarm" and its sequel "Corona Unmasked. In a recent interview with Dr. Peter Breggin, Dr. Bhakdi left no doubt: 'I say to everyone who is participating: these (mRNA) vaccines are going to change humanity.

They are going to change you - your psyche, your brain. Don't do it. You will lose your individuality and personality. You will no longer be a human being.'

Dr. Bhakdi begins the interview with a poignant message: 'I think we are in the middle of the Apocalypse. The end is near. Everyone MUST understand the danger, and stand up... against this diabolical, satanic, diabological (New World Order) agenda' of the big mega banks, multinational corporations, the military-industrial complex and international organizations such as the World Economic Forum.

In the second part of the interview, the scientist explained why, from a scientific point of view, people are easier to manipulate when they have received the mRNA injections.

He reiterated the now well-known fact that the Covid shots are not real vaccines, but trigger the human body to produce the toxic spike protein of the (supposed) coronavirus. These spikes, he believes, have only one function: to "open the door" in the cells for the virus.

The damage to the cells that ingest the mRNA is mainly caused by the body's own immune system. This too has already been confirmed in numerous scientific studies.

Once the cells start making the spike protein, the immune system will attack these cells and try to kill them. In people suffering from autoimmune diseases, exactly the same thing happens. That means injecting them with mRNA vaccines is tantamount to planting seeds for the emergence of autoimmune diseases.

'Personality people will change'

Indeed, the mRNA 'vaccines' are best compared to 'letters in an envelope,' he continued. These 'letters' travel throughout the body to unknown destinations, and are taken up by cells that the virus would never have reached. These cells are in the lymph nodes and the walls of blood vessels.

The damage done to these cells once they receive the 'letters' and carry out the instructions will be enormous; for example, numerous people have already suffered from blood clots (/ brain hemorrhages, thrombosis) and damage to the immune system itself.

'Those who have created these vaccines think they are more than God.

The 'envelope' - consisting of the lipid nanoparticles - is pure poison, as it contains toxic cationic (positively charged) lipids (fat globules). Natural lipids are negatively charged or have no charge at all.

Most of the important molecules in our cells are negatively charged. The cationic lipids bind to them and then interfere with their function. These positive lipids can even act directly on the negatively charged DNA, and also on negatively charged proteins necessary for wound healing.

Blood clots are formed wherever blood vessels are damaged. These clots can form in small vessels in places that can never be detected with scans.

Eventually, the clogging of small vessels in the brain will lead to brain damage, which will change people's personalities (either slowly or rapidly).

Pathologists found that 90% deceased people had spikes throughout their bodies

Pfizer and Moderna, according to Dr. Bhakdi, know very well that the damage to these capillaries cannot be easily detected, and think they will get away with it. Pathologists, however, can identify this damage post mortem. For example, last year German pathologists detected the spike protein in all organs, the heart, brain, liver, spleen, lungs and reproductive organs.

Their conclusion was shocking: 90% of people who died after vaccination had symptoms of an autoimmune attack, with the heart as the main target (think of the many hundreds of athletes who suddenly developed heart problems, had to quit or even died).

Numerous studies have shown that it is unpredictable how quickly that process occurs. Some people experience serious problems within days or even hours of their shot; other people can continue to function as if nothing had happened for months after their booster shot and then suddenly become seriously ill and/or die.

At the end of the interview, Dr. Breggin emphasized that "we are at a crucial moment in time. We clearly need people to courageously rise up against these things. About what you heard today: don't become helpless and get upset and overwhelmed. Get angry - but not too angry. Get to work, get active, love. Talk to your neighbors and friends... get active in local politics... Learn as much as you can and be as active as you can. We are now at a point in history where we have to stand up for freedom in the world.

'30% pilots have heart problems because of vaccines'

Another scientist who made a name for himself is cardiologist Dr. Peter McCullough. In an interview on April 20, pilot Joshua Yoder, co-founder of the transportation organization US Freedom Flyers, told tech millionaire Steve Kirsch, founder of the Vaccine Safety Research Foundation, that according to McCullough, 30% of all pilots would not pass the medical test because their hearts were affected by the Covid 'vaccines.

Yoder said that vaccinated pilots have suffered from chest pain, myocarditis and pericarditis. He personally knew at least three pilots who fly with chest pain, and another who is under treatment by a cardiologist.

Recently, American Airlines pilot Robert Snow suffered a heart attack just 6 minutes after landing at the Dallas-Fort Worth airport.

He had to be treated with a defibrillator, and was then taken to the hospital. According to Yoder, the Johnson & Johnson vaccine was the culprit. American Airlines, meanwhile, is trying to distance itself as much as possible from the incident.

Dr. Geert Vanden Bossche: NEVER take a booster shot, healthcare system will collapse

Virus and vaccine expert Dr. Geert Vanden Bossche, who once worked for the Bill & Melinda Gates Foundation and the GAVI alliance, made it to both international and our national free media with his severe criticism of vaccination policies. In November 2021, he even warned all people to "never take Covid vaccines," because they weaken the human immune system.

Earlier that year, Vanden Bossche warned that providing billions of people with new "vaccines" during a pandemic - an absolute no go in immunology until 2020 - would have dire consequences because it could make the mutations that normally always occur, especially of respiratory viruses such as corona, much more dangerous.

He later urged anyone who did get vaccinated not to take a booster shot under any circumstances, because it is "absolutely insane. Booster shots actually put even more pressure on the natural immune system. 'This is dangerous and should not be done.' If boostered people come into contact with all kinds of diseases at some point, what is left of their immune system will have extreme difficulty protecting the body anymore.

Consequently, most vaccinated people, but especially those who are born, will at some point require "intensive medical treatment.

At the same time, the immune system of the unvaccinated will actually become more and more powerful. But since the vast majority of people have been vaccinated and boostered, 'this will inevitably lead to the collapse of our healthcare system. I'm not a doomsday preacher, but it can't be said any other way.'

Sudden adult death syndrome?

Over 45,000 vax deaths and 2 million seriously and/or permanently ill and disabled in EU still ignored by medical community - *Released documents prove Pfizer knew children could get Vaccine Syndrome*

Sudden Adult Death Syndrome (SADS) is the latest excuse the medical community is trying to explain away the huge number of supposedly "unexpected" younger victims of the Covid-19 "vaccine" victims with.

People under 40 are being advised to have their hearts checked because many are said to be at risk of Sudden Adult Death Syndrome, or SADS for short. The syndrome can be fatal for all types of people, regardless of their lifestyle and health.

The large numbers of hemispherically different young(er) people who suddenly drop dead - including hundreds of top-flight athletes - arguably have only one thing in common, and that is that almost without exception they have been vaccinated against Covid-19.

But since the mRNA gene manipulation injections have been declared sacrosanct, they should never be blamed.

That would also immediately kill numerous international politicians and medical leaders.

Road map of vax victims predicted by 2020

103

That is why The Royal Australian College of General Practioners is also saying nothing about the injections. SADS, according to the doctors' organization, is merely "an umbrella term to describe unexpected deaths in young people. SADS primarily affects people under 40.

Declaring vax victims away to some new disease or syndrome is something we predicted as far back as 2020, by the way.

SADS is diagnosed when post-mortem no obvious cause of death can be found. The SADS Foundation in the U.S. claims that more than half of the 4,000 annual SADS victims among children, teens and young adults have at least one of the two main warning signs.

These include a family history of unexpected deaths, and fainting or seizures during physical exertion, excitement, or tenseness.

The example given is 31-year-old Catherine Keane, who reportedly died in her sleep last year in Dublin. Her mother stated that Keane was top fit, walked 10,000 steps every day and went to the gym.

'Advice: get your heart checked as soon as possible'

In Australia, the first official registry of SADS victims is now being developed. According to the Baker Heart and Diabetes Institute in Melbourne, about 750 people under 50 have heart attacks each year in the state of

Victoria. No cause of death is found in about 100 younger persons, even after an extensive autopsy.

Cardiologist Dr. Elizabeth Paratz explains the previous lack of attention to SADS to the fact that "a lot takes place outside the traditional medical setting" and "90% of these SADS cases take place outside the hospital," which is patently a bullshit argument, especially since one extremely relative reason for it has been identified since early last year: the "vaccination" of the entire population against Covid-19.

According to Dr. Paratz, combating SADS is difficult, as scientists have still not been able to find the 'genes' that supposedly cause SADS. Her "best advice" to anyone with an unexpected and unexplained death in their family is to get their heart checked as soon as possible.

Over 45,000 Covid vax deaths in the EU

Doctors and other medics could, of course, just look at the official statistics to see the real cause of the SADS explosion.

According to the European Medicines Agency's monitor, EudraVigilance, 45,316 people have already died in the EU from Covid-19 injections, more than 4.4 million people have been sickened, a scant half of them (nearly 2 million) seriously and/or permanently, including disabilities such as paralysis and blindness.

In the US, the figures are no less frightening. For example, 37,301 children between 12 and 18 have already become (seriously) ill or died after being injected with a Covid 'vaccine'. About 12% of the victims (3809 cases) are from California.

 That doesn't stop this left-liberal state from wanting to vaccinate children between 12 and 18 against Covid-19 without their parents' consent. The California legislature will decide on that this week. Incidentally, children in the state have already been allowed to decide for themselves to have the highly harmful HPV vaccine injected since 2011.

Pfizer and FDA knew children could get Vaccine Syndrome

Several U.S. doctors noted on behalf of the University of Colorado that children could get Vaccine Associated Enhanced Disease (V-AED). A closer analysis of confidential Pfizer documents that had to be released after a court order shows that both the manufacturer and the FDA (Food & Drug Administration) knew this was going to happen.

The very purpose of the study was to prove that the Covid injections would protect children from MIS (Multisystem Inflammatory Syndrome). Unfortunately, the doctors discovered that the "vaccines" do the exact opposite, and actually cause MIS.

All in all, one of the all-time greatest crimes in human history, injecting billions of people with experimental gene manipulation 'vaccines' under the guise of fighting a virus that has proven to be no more dangerous than the flu, continues. Even young children have been made guinea pigs of the pharmaceutical complex, which seems to have taken complete control of Western politicians in particular.